before th·

The Theatre Makers

How Seven Great Artists Shaped the Modern Theatre

Helping You to Achieve

The Theatre Makers

How Seven Great Artists Shaped the Modern Theatre

David Chadderton

ISBN: 978-1-84285-083-1

First published by Studymates Limited, PO Box 225, Abergele, LL18 9AY,
United Kingdom.

Website: http://www.studymates.co.uk

Typeset by Vikatan Publishing Solutions, Chennai, India
Printed and bound in Europe

Contents

Introduction   ix

1 Konstantin Stanislavski   1
Biography Overview   1
Theory and Practice   5
   Stanislavski's legacy   5
Training the Actor   6
   Relaxation   7
   Action   8
      Given Circumstances   9
      If   10
   Concentration of attention   10
      Object of Attention   10
      Circles of Attention   12
   Imagination   14
   Emotion Memory   16
   Communion   19
   Adaptation   20
   Tempo-rhythm   21
      Speech Tempo-rhythm   23
The 'System' in Rehearsal   24
   Preliminary analysis   25
      Supertask   25
      Through-action and
         Counter-through-action   25
   Breaking down the play   26
      Episodes, Basic Actions, Tasks, Facts   26
      Subtext   26
   The text   27
   Preparing the production   27
   Sample Questions   28

2 Edward Gordon Craig   29
Biography Overview   29
Theory and Practice   33
   A question of style   33

The stage director 36
Craig and the actor 38
Stage design 42
The Steps 42
Screens 44
Sample Questions 47

3 Antonin Artaud   49
Biography Overview 49
Theory and Practice 52
The language of theatre 52
Theatre of Cruelty 55
A Theatre of Cruelty production 57
Content 57
Staging 58
Direction 60
Performers 60
Set 60
Lighting 60
Sound 62
Costume 63
Sample Questions 64

4 Bertolt Brecht   65
Biography Overview 65
Theory and Practice 67
Epic theatre 67
Dialectics 71
Dialectical Materialism 72
Dialectical Theatre 73
Alienation 75
Gest 78
Lehrstücke 80
Model books 82
Couragemodell 84
Sample Questions 90

5 Jerzy Grotowski   91
Biography Overview 91
Theory and Practice 95

Poor Theatre   95
    Training the Actor   97
    The Actor's Role   102
    Text   105
    Performance space   108
Sample Questions   111

6 **Peter Brook**   **113**
Biography Overview   113
Theory and Practice   117
    The empty space   117
    The four theatres   122
        The Deadly Theatre   122
        The Holy Theatre   126
        The Rough Theatre   129
        The Immediate Theatre   131
Sample Questions   135

7 **Augusto Boal**   **137**
Biography Overview   137
Theory and Practice   141
    Theatre of the Oppressed   141
        First Stage: Knowing the Body   142
        Second Stage: Making the Body
                          Expressive   143
        Third Stage: The Theatre as Language   143
        Fourth Stage: The Theatre as Discourse 147
Sample Questions   153

Further Reference   155

Glossary of Terms   167

Index   171

Introduction

The seven theatre artists looked at in the following chapters were all practical men of the theatre (two of them, Peter Brook and Augusto Boal, are still alive and still producing work) who dedicated their lives to working with actors and putting productions on stage. Between them they also produced a substantial amount of theoretical work, which helps to explain their theatre work and the context in which it was produced, as well as documenting the methods they used to create it. Theatre, however, is the most ephemeral of all art forms, and so for most of these great artists the productions have long gone and the theories are all that remain. The people who produced some of the most innovative and exciting drama of the twentieth century are therefore often thought of as dull theoreticians whose work is difficult to understand, outdated and impossible to implement in real productions. The work that they produced themselves and their continuing influence on theatre, film, television, education, politics, popular culture, rock concerts, drug culture and many other areas of modern life would seem to contradict this idea.

The aim of this book is to bring the practice and the theory back together, using practical examples to aid understanding of the theoretical principles. Some of the exercises used here have been taken or adapted from ones used by the practitioners; others have been specially devised to clarify a particular concept. Many of these theories were created after practical experiments, and so the exercises in this book use practical experiments to try to discover what they were trying to achieve and how they achieved it. Trying out the methods of these practitioners will bring a much deeper understanding of what they were trying to achieve than just reading about their work.

The writings of all of the people covered show that they all had a detailed knowledge of the theatre of their own time and of theatre history; without this knowledge they would not have had such a clear image of what they were reacting against or what they were working towards in their own ideal theatre. They all saw serious deficiencies in the theatre of their own time and believed they had the answer to creating a better theatre for the future. Many of them were also influenced by one another: Boal acknowledges the influence of both Brecht and Stanislavski on his work; Brook has worked from Artaud's theories and once brought Grotowski in to work with his actors; the ghosts of Stanislavski and Artaud can be found in Grotowski's work. The artists who create the most significant theatre of the future will only do so with knowledge of the achievements of the greatest artists from the past and present.

Another feature common to all of these practitioners is their great attention to detail. Many of them rehearsed for months or even years before putting a production before an audience; Grotowski would even take productions off and rework them, or work on something for months and then never show it. Any recreation of their work, if it is to have any value, must show a similar attention to detail, and so it is important to spend time working through the exercises in order to understand their work properly. There are many myths and misunderstandings about all of these artists that have come about because of incomplete knowledge of their work and half-hearted implementations of their ideas. This book attempts to correct some of the misunderstandings and show the immense achievements and continuing relevance of these great theatre makers.

There are a few people I would like to thank for their help and support during the writing of this book. Firstly thanks to Paul Heap of Tormead School in Guildford, Chris Megson of Royal Holloway College University of London in Egham and Anthony Hozier, Vice Principal of Rose Bruford College in Sidcup, for their advice and encouragement from the initial proposal to the final manuscript. A great deal of thanks must also go to Barry Carr of Mainstream Theatre Arts for giving me encouragement and time to complete the project. Finally, this book could not have been completed without the support of Lindsey Wright, whose assistance has covered so many areas from finding research materials, to encouraging me to write when I was finding it difficult, to pointing out my mistakes and those sentences that made sense only to me.

1 Konstantin Stanislavski

Biography Overview

Konstantin Sergeievich Alekseiev, later to become Konstantin Stanislavski, was born on 5 January 1863, the second of ten children to one of the richest families in Russia. He was brought up in a fashionable district of Moscow at a time when Russian painting, theatre, opera, literature and ballet were flourishing, and he and his brothers and sisters were taken to the theatre and to concerts from an early age. Stanislavski's cousin by marriage spent a lot of his money on mounting theatre and opera performances and concerts, and many of Russia's top actors, dancers, writers and musicians were friends of his family. Stanislavski's favourite entertainment, though, was the circus. The children would often re-enact scenes from performances they had seen, either playing the parts themselves or using puppets.

In 1877, Stanislavski's father converted one of his outbuildings into a fully equipped theatre. Stanislavski appeared in two of the four opening performances, and he began a habit of making detailed notes about his acting performances that he kept up for the rest of his life. After he left school and joined the family business, his father converted two rooms in the house into a second theatre with 300 seats and plush decor where Stanislavski could devote all of his spare time to creating performances. Here he began to develop various techniques and exercises for getting his actors to play their parts with increased realism. However, whilst Konstantin Alekseiev, respected businessman, gained favourable reviews for his amateur performances of quality plays, Stanislavski began to appear in less respectable plays and venues. Acting was not considered a respectable profession, especially for someone of his status, and so he adopted the name Stanislavski, inherited from a friend and fellow amateur who, like him, was an admirer of the ballerina Stanislavskaia, in order to hide his double life from his parents. The secret was revealed when he walked on stage to see his mother and father in the audience. His father said he didn't mind him acting in a proper dramatic circle, but he should 'stop appearing in muck with God knows who'.

In 1888, against the advice of his family and friends, he spent a large amount of his wealth on setting up the Society of Art and Literature, an organisation with an attached school which brought together artists of all kinds. While performing for the Society under the direction of Aleksandr Fedotov, who had acted at the Mali with the great Mikhaïl Shchepkin, Stanislavski made some of his greatest breakthroughs as an actor, creating characters from his own personality rather than copying gestures from other actors. In 1889 he married Lilina—she, too, used an acting pseudonym because she was from a respectable family and was actually Maria Petrovna Perevostchikova—whom he had acted with a number of times.

In 1893, after the deaths of his father and brother Stanislavski became head of the family business. He was a very successful businessman and a popular employer, but he was unhappy in this role as he only wanted to create theatre. On 22 June 1897, Stanislavski and the playwright Vladimir Ivanovich Nemirovich-Danchenko had an eighteen-hour meeting, ending at eight o'clock the next morning, during which they agreed to set up an Art Theatre with an ensemble of actors and with affordable ticket prices. Nemirovich would have control of the repertoire, Stanislavski the staging of the plays. The Open Art Theatre—soon to become the Moscow Art Theatre—opened on 14 October 1898 with Tolstoi's *Tsar Fiodor Ioannovich*, which was a great success, but the next few plays were disastrous failures. The theatre's fortunes were saved in December, however, by the spectacular success of Chekhov's *The Seagull*. The company began building a repertoire of productions of new and old plays, some of which were considered politically subversive by the authorities. Each was based on a detailed '*mis-en-scène*',worked out by Stanislavski in advance, specifying every move, gesture, pause, tone of voice and sound effect.

In 1902, Stanislavski began writing down ideas about a 'grammar' of acting, which eventually formed the basis for *An Actor's Work on Himself*. In 1905, he wrote of his doubts about the Art Theatre's established system of giving the actors a detailed plan at the first rehearsal. He set up the experimental Theatre-Studio in collaboration with the actor Vsevolod Meierhold, but it failed and was closed. The political situation in Russia was deteriorating after the failed Bolshevik revolution in October 1905, and so the Art Theatre's company set out on its first foreign tour which spread the company's reputation throughout Europe.

Stanislavski began to experiment more seriously with making the actor, rather than the director, at the centre of the rehearsal process, using improvisation and exercises to explore characters and situations. Some company members, including Nemirovich, regarded Stanislavski's new methods as ridiculous and disruptive. Actors who had been used to performing moves and gestures given to them by the director found it difficult to adapt to having to look for the character's motivation behind every move for themselves. In 1909 and 1910, he experimented with his methods and schooled his actors during rehearsals for *A Month in the Country* and *Hamlet* (co-directed and designed by Edward Gordon Craig). He now considered that real theatre could only be created by an ensemble of artists working together, not by a company dominated by an author or a star actor.

In 1912, Stanislavski founded the First Studio with a group of actors with professional experience who were not old enough to be set in their ways. These actors, among them Richard Boleslavski, Evgeni Vakhtangov and Michael Chekhov, had to attend classes and put together their own productions, as well as attending rehearsals and performing in productions for the main Arts Theatre company. Stanislavski also used rehearsals for the main company's productions to teach his 'system'.

In February 1917, Tsar Nicholas II was forcibly removed from power. Stanislavski broadly supported the overthrow of an oppressive government, but the revolution put his factory into state ownership and lost him his private fortune. The Art Theatre was given official status, but some members of the new government did not support the theatre. Stanislavski and others were arrested at one point, suspected of being anti-Bolshevik. He continued to teach his techniques in the Studios, and in 1918 set up an Opera Studio with young singers from the Bolshoi and Moscow Conservatoire, partly to show that his system could be employed beyond naturalistic plays. When he was evicted from his home by the authorities in 1921, Lenin found him a property near to the Art Theatre that provided both living accommodation and space for his Opera Studio. He lived here for the rest of his life. The following year, Stanislavski's famous staging of Tchaikovski's *Evgeni Onegin* with the Opera Studio opened, and the Art Theatre took some of its most famous productions on tour around Europe and America. Boleslavski, with Stanislavski's permission, gave a series of lectures in America on the 'system', which were later published. Whilst in America, Stanislavski began reluctantly to write his biography *My Life In Art* in order to pay for his son Igor's treatment for tuberculosis. This was finally published in 1924 in a poor, rushed translation.

In 1928, Stanislavski suffered a massive heart attack whilst playing Vershinin in an excerpt of *Three Sisters* at a gala for the Art Theatre's jubilee. He managed to finish the scene and take two curtain calls before going off, but this event signalled the end of his acting career. However, he continued to work on production plans for plays and operas and to put together his notes and exercises on his 'system' for publication. The 'Method of Physical Actions' was developed, and *An Actor's Work On Himself*—translated into English as *An Actor Prepares*—became the first of his works to explain and teach Stanislavski's 'system'. Frustrated by the divisions in the Arts Theatre, Stanislavski set up the Opera-Dramatic Studio to pass on his techniques in 1935. By 1938, he had revised *An Actor's Work On Himself: Part One* for Russian publication, but he died on 2 August. *An Actor's Work On Himself: Part Two* and *An Actor's Work On*

A Role were unfinished, and his notes were not compiled into published works (in English *Building A Character* and *Creating A Role*) for many years.

Theory and Practice

Stanislavski's legacy

Stanislavski was, by all accounts, an extremely talented actor and a director with great vision and imagination. However, his most significant legacy is undoubtedly his acting 'system', which has had a significant influence on the way actors all over the world have worked ever since.

The young Stanislavski found Russian theatre to be filled with acting clichés. Actors repeated standard gestures for each type of situation, and even the most talented actors could not rely on inspiration to strike every time, just when they needed it. What was needed was a new approach to acting that created each character afresh as though they were a real person, together with reliable techniques for the actor to awaken his creativity just when he needed it. This should not simply be a set of new rules, as these would soon become as tired and clichéd as the ones they had replaced; it had to be a set of techniques for helping the actor to create new rules that only apply to them in that role in that production of that play. Stanislavski always wrote about his 'system' with lowercase 's' and in quote marks to indicate that it is not a fixed set of rules and was constantly being revised.

Stanislavski only saw two works through to publication during his lifetime. The autobiographical *My Life In Art* was, he admitted, rushed and contains many inaccuracies. His first book to explain the 'system', *The Actor's Work On Himself*, was split into two volumes, only the first of which was completed before he died. This was translated into English as *An Actor Prepares* and then cut down by a further half by the translator and editor, neither of whom had any real knowledge of the 'system', before publication. Stanislavski's most famous work is therefore only a quarter of what he intended it to be. The later books, *Building A Character* and *Creating A Role*, were compiled from the many notes and proposed chapters left behind when Stanislavski died and published many years later. These books are still useful descriptions of elements of the 'system' but they are far from complete.

To add to the confusion, the popular version of the 'system' that spread in America came from the teachings of Stanislavski's former student Richard Boleslavski, who was unaware of later developments in the 'system' and chose to focus on techniques of emotion memory that Stanislavski had abandoned. Stanislavski taught American actress Stella Adler for five weeks in 1934, and she caused great controversy when she reported back to Lee Strasberg (student of Boleslavski and founder of the Method) and the Group Theatre in New York of his emphasis on physical actions rather than emotion memory.

How are we to learn about the Stanislavski 'system' if we cannot rely on any of the published material?

Towards the end of his life, Stanislavski realised that he would not live to see a comprehensive description of his 'system' in print. He therefore set up another studio and picked twenty students out of over three thousand auditionees to teach his system to in a comprehensive four-year training course. Many of these students kept copious notes on their classes, and these provide the clearest guide of how Stanislavski saw his techniques being taught and practised after sixty years of experimentation.

Training the Actor

The following are some of the most important techniques that Stanislavski used for training actors. He used everyday words for his techniques so that actors would not have to learn new jargon terms, but this simplicity of language has not always survived the translation from Russian. As well as classes in acting, Stanislavski's students would have to attend classes in voice, physical training, stage combat and repertoire so that their bodies, voices and minds were flexible and responsive enough to be able to express the thoughts and emotions of their characters and communicate them to an audience.

Relaxation

Muscular tension can restrict the actor physically, emotionally and vocally. Some tension is necessary to move and retain physical positions, but although tensing your body can make you feel as though you are giving an emotional performance, you are not in control of your body and so your movements can appear stiff and robotic. This lack of control can even be dangerous; the chapter on relaxation in *An Actor Prepares* begins with an incident where Kostia tenses his hand so much that he breaks an object under his hand and loses so much blood that he has to spend the next few days in bed.

Relaxing muscles
Lie on the floor on your back and close your eyes. Try to feel which muscles in your body are tense and relax them. You may find that when you relax one muscle, tension appears somewhere else. Spend time working on your whole body to free it from tension, particularly in the shoulders, neck and back, and not forgetting the face.

Necessary tension
Stand upright with your hands by your sides. Feel where the tensions are in your muscles and relax them so that they are only as tense as they need to be to hold you upright.

Very slowly, raise and lower one arm. Feel which muscles tense up, and if they are not working to move your arm, relax them completely before continuing. Do the same with the other arm.

Walk around the room, feeling which muscles tense up more than necessary and relaxing them as you move.

Perform various kinds of physical activities—such as unpacking items from a box, setting the table, cleaning a room—all the while concentrating on which muscles become tense at different moments and relaxing those that are not essential to the movement or position.

> Spend time on all of these exercises—they should not be rushed if you are to benefit from them—and repeat them regularly.

Action

In *An Actor Prepares*, the Director gave one of his students the following play to perform:

> The curtain goes up, and you are sitting on the stage. You are alone. You sit and sit and sit. ... At last the curtain comes down again. That is the whole play.

> **Sitting on stage**
> One at a time, perform the above play in front of your group. If you can, raise and lower a curtain or lights—even if it is just the main room light—to signal the beginning and end of the play, which must last at least two to three minutes.

What were your performances like? They almost certainly would have fell into the following two categories:

a. The actor appears nervous and conscious of being watched and is unable to perform even the simplest of moves naturally.
b. The actor tries to find things to do that are interesting for the audience to watch instead of behaving naturally.

Stanislavski's explanation for this is that these actions had no purpose, something he believed every action performed on stage should have.

> **Motivated action**
> Perform the same play, but this time you are sitting because:
>
> a. You are outside the office of a senior manager, college principal or head teacher. You have been summoned

there and do not know why, but can only think it must have been because you did something really bad.

b. You have had some really exciting news (decide what it is). You are sat waiting for your friend and cannot wait to tell them.

c. You have to make a life-changing decision in the next few minutes (decide what this is). You sit down for a moment to consider your options before making that decision.

d. You can hear something happening in the next room that makes you frightened of being discovered listening (decide what you can hear).

Play the situation as if it was happening to you in real life, not to entertain, amuse or impress your audience.

Here, all actions are justified with a purpose, and so they immediately become more natural and more interesting to watch.

But how can you talk of action when the situations in the last exercise involved hardly any movement?

To Stanislavski, action was not just physical movement. In some situations, the inner action of a character could be far greater than any external movement (although there must be some external signs of this for it to be communicated to an audience). He wrote, 'On the stage, you must always be enacting something; action, motion, is the basis of the art followed by the actor.' This action may involve little or no physical movement.

Given Circumstances

Each time you act something out, you will be given some information beforehand. For an improvisation, this may be a prop, a location or a basic action. When acting in a play, you will have the dialogue and stage directions in the script, the interpretation of the director, scenery, costumes, music, sound effects and lighting. The actor must incorporate all of these things into his or her performance and justify them in the character and their behaviour. This prior information is called the Given Circumstances.

If

'If'—sometimes referred to as 'Magic If' or 'What If'—works hand-in-hand with the Given Circumstances to bring life to a scene. The principle of 'If' goes straight to the contradiction at the heart of the actor's job: I have to appear to be someone else in a situation that may be unfamiliar to me while knowing that beneath the costume and make-up I am still me surrounded by painted flats with an audience watching me. I can never become that other person and experience their thoughts and feelings directly (Stanislavski said that anyone who believes that they *are* someone else needs psychiatric help) so apart from the Given Circumstances I only have my own memories and experiences to draw upon. 'If' can provide the bridge between these personal experiences and the fictional experiences of the character: I know I am me on a stage set, but *if* I was in a real room and there was a psychotic killer outside with an axe (an exercise from *An Actor Prepares*) what would *I* do; how would *I* feel and react? The answer to this can be used as a basis for the character's actions. Stanislavski believed that for a performance to appear real, the actor must use his or her own experiences and instincts; therefore each actor will create a slightly different portrayal of the same character from identical Given Circumstances.

Concentration of attention

Stanislavski believed that the actor's focus of attention should always be somewhere on the stage, never in the auditorium. The eye of the spectator is drawn to look where the actor looks, and if the actor's attention is not on the stage, the spectator's attention may follow.

Object of Attention

If you find your attention wandering into the auditorium, one way of getting it back onto the stage is to focus on a nearby object. However, looking at something on stage as though you are really looking at it, and as if you find it interesting, takes some practice.

Examining an object

Scatter some objects around the room. Half of the group should each sit facing an object, spending time to really look and examine it, taking in every detail. The remaining group members should watch them. How convinced are you that they are really looking at the objects with genuine interest? Are some of them looking in the direction of the object without appearing to be really looking at it at all? Are some making their eyes pop out to try to convince you that they are looking at the object? Are some looking at the object just as an interested person would in real life? Swap over the two halves and repeat.

Object of Attention

Create a solo scene that involves close attention to an object, for instance:

- Opening a present (What is it? Who is it from? Is it a surprise?)
- Counting money (Whose is it? Why have you got it?)
- Opening a letter (Who is it from? What does it say? Are you expecting it?)
- Examining information on a computer (What do you want to know? How badly?)
- Arrange some flowers (Who are they from?)
- Change the film in a camera (What type of film and camera? Where are you going with it? What are you going to photograph?)
- Mending something (What is it? What is wrong with it? How did it happen?)

Play the scene as truthfully as possible using all of your senses, not just sight, where appropriate. Do you find your attention wandering from your task to see what others are doing, to see the reactions of spectators or just into your thoughts? If so, make a special effort to find something of interest in your object to refocus your attention on your task.

Circles of Attention

At any moment, a person's attention is concentrated on a particular area. A person on a high mountain observing the view would try to take in the whole of the surrounding area as far as they can see. That same person cooking a meal in a small kitchen would have their attention focused on a much smaller area, such as a pan or cutting board. Stanislavski referred to the area of the actor's focus as the Circle of Attention, which can be small (for instance, a table top), medium (part of the room), large (the whole room) or largest (as far as the eye can see). On stage, the actors are always in a public place observed by an audience, however intimate their actions, but they need to achieve what Stanislavski referred to as Solitude in Public—an appearance of privacy and intimacy whilst before an audience.

Circles of Attention

Create the following scenes with various sized Circles of Attention, trying not to let your attention wander outside this circle.

Small Circle of Attention:

- Prepare the ingredients for a meal on a worktop (What is it? Who is it for? What is the occasion, if any?)
- Search through a drawer in a filing cabinet for a particular document (What is the document? Why can you not find it? Should you be looking for it?)

Medium Circle of Attention:

- You have to create a display to fill one wall of the room (What kind of display? What for? Who for?)
- You are sat at a table eating dinner with guests (Who are they? What is the dinner in aid of? Do you need to impress them?)

Large Circle of Attention:

- You are in a public place but believe you are being followed (Why do you think this? Who by? What do you think they will do to you?)
- You are supervising the layout of a room for an important function (What is the function? Who is it for? Who are you in relation to it?)
- You walk into a room you have never been in before and are amazed by the room (What impresses you about it? Where are you? Why are you there?)
- You walk into a room that you know and find that everything in it is different from how you remember (What is different about it? Why has it been changed? How does it make you feel?)

During a scene, it is likely that the area occupying your attention will change; one minute you may be examining an object closely, the next you may be addressing a roomful of people. It is therefore important to practice expanding and contracting the circle without your focus wandering from the stage. Larger circles are more difficult to focus on, and so Stanislavski recommended shrinking your Circle of Attention if you feel you are losing focus until you get it back, then expanding it slowly again. It is also difficult to keep focus when your circle is not near to you, for instance, if you are focused on someone or something at the other side of the room or through a window.

Changing Focus
Create the following scenes, and then make up some scenes of your own that will let you practice changing focus.

- You are in a small bookshop. Look around the shop for the section that has the book you want (large circle). Look for the shelf that has the type of book that you want (medium circle). Go along that shelf to find your book (small circle). Take your book and examine it (object).

- You find a wallet on the floor in a public place. You examine the wallet and find a card with the owner's photo on it (object). You look at the person nearest to where you found it, but that isn't them (small circle). You widen your search to the group of people in that area (medium circle) and finally you look all around you to find the person in the photo (large circle).

Imagination

Imagination is the actor's tool for creating believable characters and behaviour from the Given Circumstances. Stanislavski believed that the imagination could be developed with appropriate exercises.

The Chairs
Place a chair in the centre of the room. Playing the scene truthfully, not for laughs, sit on the chair as though it is:

- a hot stove
- an electric chair for executions
- a seat in a roller coaster
- the dentist's chair
- a seat in a waiting room for a job interview
- a chair at home when you have been walking around all day
- a chair at home, and a policeman has arrived and asked you to sit down
- a seat in a shoe shop
- the chair in your new office after your promotion

The simplest way to begin work on the imagination is to take a familiar situation that is largely true and change something to see how it is affected.

Imagination—changing your situation
As a group, imagine you are exactly where you are but shift the time forward twelve hours, so if it is three o'clock in the afternoon, imagine it is three o'clock the

next morning. What "if" it was three in the morning? Why might you be there at that time? (Perhaps you have an examination or a performance the next day and must rehearse, or you have been locked in by mistake.) Where should you have been by now? What have you missed that you were going to do? Who will be missing you? Can you get a message to them? How are you going to get home? Do you have money for a bus or taxi? Can you get a bus at this time? Work out every little detail, do not generalise anything, and play the scene.

This time, you are exactly where you are but six months from now, so if it is now midwinter, it becomes midsummer. What would be different "if" the seasons had changed? Would it be lighter or darker? Would you feel any different? Would something exciting have just happened, or be just about to (such as a holiday or Christmas)? Would you be dressed differently?

Stanislavski stressed that the imagination must fill in every tiny detail for it to have any value to the actor. An imagined scenario without these details is only imagined 'in general' and is of no value. A script will often give only the vaguest description of a character's actions, and the actor must fill in all the details (Where have they come from? Why are they there? How do they enter?) in order to perform the scene convincingly.

Imagination—creating an imagined scenario

Take it in turns for one person to imagine and another to question. The person imagining may find it easier to close their eyes. The questioner is there to prompt and help their partner, not to catch them out.

Imaginer: Imagine yourself in a specific place (you should start with a place you know well, but later you can try to create a place from your imagination). Look around you. What do you see? What do you hear? What happens? What do you do? Describe everything in great detail.

Questioner: Your job is to get your partner to describe everything they 'see' in detail and not to generalise about anything. If they see a table, what is it made of? What colour is it? Where in the room does it stand? What is on it, or under it? If they stand in a field, what type of field? What colour is it? What is in the field? If you can, persuade them into action so that their imagined scene doesn't remain passive. Why are they here? What are they going to do here? If they see a letter, get them to read it and then act on what they read. If they hear a noise downstairs, do they hide or investigate?

Emotion Memory

As has been noted previously, Emotion Memory was a controversial topic even during Stanislavski's lifetime. He undoubtedly used it—a substantial chapter is devoted to it in *An Actor Prepares*, although even here he talks of the importance of external stimuli such as scenery, lighting and sound in helping the actor to create the right emotion—but his later 'system' depended rather less on it than the methods of other teachers who were inspired by him. Emotion Memory uses the actor's memories of past events to trigger physical actions to communicate their remembered feelings to an audience. It has, however, been overused by some teachers and actors, resulting in introverted, isolated performances and some distressed acting students.

Emotion Memories

Try to remember in detail a time when you experienced the following, examining what you did and how you felt:

- You were having a really good time
- You were really frightened
- Someone gave you a present unexpectedly
- Something made you really angry
- Something made you really happy
- Somebody did something that really amazed you
- You were bored

- You were jealous of somebody
- You were excited about something
- You experienced the death of a person or pet close to you
- You were ashamed about something you had done
- You were sad about something
- You desired revenge on someone
- You met an old friend you hadn't seen for a long time
- You met someone you didn't like
- You were really embarrassed

Linked with Emotion Memory and sometimes of use for triggering it is Sensory (or Sensation) Memory, where we are able to bring to mind something from the past that we have seen, heard, touched, tasted or smelled. These sensations sometimes have associations with events from our past that can trigger emotional recall.

Sensory Memory

Try to recall in detail any of the following that you have actually experienced:

The sight of:

- a house where you used to live
- a park or woodland
- the face of someone you are close to
- a place you like to visit
- a famous building
- a supermarket
- an evening sky

The sound of:

- the dawn chorus
- children playing in the park
- traffic on a busy road
- music at a concert
- footsteps on concrete, gravel or snow

- waves and seagulls at the seaside
- animals at the zoo

The taste of:

- chocolate
- a medicine you took as a child
- ice cream
- pizza
- sugar
- lemons

The smell of:

- bread or cakes being baked
- a wet dog
- the countryside after it has rained
- smoke from a bonfire
- a new book
- hot tar being used for road repairs
- freshly cut grass

The feel of:

- a soft pillow
- a powerful shower
- stroking an animal
- sandpaper
- your clothes stuck to you with sweat when it is hot
- wrapping yourself in a thick jumper when it is cold
- wet sand between your toes on the beach

If I can only draw on experiences I have had in real life for my acting, surely this restricts the types of parts I can play?

You do not have to have had precisely the same experience, but it is likely you have had an experience that triggered a similar emotion in you, even if it wasn't to the same degree. For instance, it is unlikely that an actor playing Hamlet has an uncle who murdered his father and married his mother, but he will certainly have had experiences that have made him angry at someone and want revenge that he can draw on to inform the actions of his character. When a sumptuous medieval banquet is actually painted papier mâché created by the props department, the memory of a fantastic meal you once had can help you to react as though you really desire this fake food.

Emotion Memory in rehearsal
Take a character from a play that you are rehearsing or studying. Go through every scene, noting down the emotions that your character goes through at every point in the play. Also note down experiences that you have had in your own life that have triggered similar emotions. Do not just concentrate on the extreme emotional moments; each character is experiencing some emotion at every moment.

Communion

According to Stanislavski, we are all in communion—or communication—with something or someone at every moment. This is most obvious when you are in conversation with someone, but you can communicate without words, or you can be in communion with an object, with music, or with your own thoughts. An actor must be aware of what or whom his character is in communion with at every moment. It is not uncommon to see actors who only act when they are speaking, but if you watch two people having a conversation in real life, you can see exchanges between them even when neither of them is speaking.

The most obvious form of communication is *verbal*. The words we use, usually taken from the script, and the way we say these words communicates our message. Often accompanying the words but also sometimes used without speech is *gestural* communication. Movements of our hands, arms or even our whole body go to emphasise, elaborate, contextualise, contradict or take the place of spoken communication. A third form Stanislavski referred to as *radiation*, sending rays, where we seem to read each other's thoughts by interpreting almost imperceptible moves and changes in expression.

Sending rays

Sit facing a partner and take it in turns to 'send rays' to one another. The communicator should just think of their message without trying consciously to change their expression or to make their thoughts obvious. The observer's task is twofold:

a. to guess the message in their partner's mind;
b. to observe whether their partner is relaxed and natural or tense and trying to force their expressions in order to transmit their message.

First of all, think of an attitude you may have towards your partner. For instance, you may regard them with affection, jealousy, respect, disdain, hatred, amusement, frustration, shame. You may find it easier to hold a conversation with one another while performing the exercise.

Secondly, repeat the Emotion Memories exercise, choosing one of the memories at random and thinking of it. Again, your partner has to guess what type of thoughts you are having and watch for unnecessary tension and forced expressions.

Adaptation

On stage, as in real life, if we have a task to do, such as writing a letter, we may be able to do it without any difficulty. However, we may encounter an obstacle, for instance, our pen may run out of ink, or somebody may have forbidden us to contact the person we wish to write to, or the last post will be collected in five minutes. In order to achieve our goal of writing a letter we have to use Adaptations in order to overcome these obstacles.

Adaptations

Play the following scenes, creating Adaptations to overcome the obstacles given.

- Ask someone for directions, BUT
    i. they are hard of hearing.

> ii. it is pouring with rain and they are keen to get away.
> iii. they have a fierce dog which has taken a dislike to you.
> - You have to study for an important exam tomorrow, BUT
>   i. the person you live with insists on listening to loud music.
>   ii. the cleaner is vacuuming and wants to get the cleaning finished now.
>   iii. your electricity has been cut off and it is getting dark.

Tempo-rhythm

When he was working with his students in his Opera Studio, Stanislavski looked at how much influence the structure of the music had on the way an opera was acted. The pace of a scene, the speed of delivery of the words, even the pauses are all dictated rigidly by the music, giving opera performers a much more solid structure to create the mood of a scene than actors have in a play.

Stanislavski created the name Tempo-rhythm from two different, but related, musical terms. Tempo is the overall speed of the music or scene; rhythm is the arrangement of beats, notes, words or actions within that tempo. Certain actions will only seem right with a particular tempo and rhythm; a bride racing down the aisle at a gallop or an army marching to an irregular rhythm would seem like something from a comedy show.

Varying the tempo

You are a waiter serving everyone else in the room. Start up a regular rhythm—preferably from a metronome if you have one, but, if not, someone can clap it out—of approximately one beat every two seconds. Perform the scene, but only carrying out one simple action (one step, one move, one gesture) for each beat. Why might you be moving at this slow tempo? Fill in the details to justify your actions. Perhaps you are old and unable to walk very well, or the room is full of obstacles you must step over, or maybe someone is making a speech and you are trying to be quiet. Now double the tempo and repeat the scene. How does this change the action? Create a new background story to accompany your new tempo. Now double the tempo again and change your story. Keep doubling the tempo for as long as you can keep up with it.

Do the same thing with different actions, for instance:

- getting ready to go out
- searching for something
- tidying up
- walking home

Varying the rhythm

Go back to the waiter scene, but set the tempo at one beat per second. Divide every second beat into two, so your count is 'one, two-and-one, two-and-one...', and justify the change of rhythm. Why do you perform twice as many actions on one beat than on the previous beat? Are you clumsy? Drunk? Limping? Now at the same tempo, divide every fourth beat into four, counting 'one, two, three, four-and-and-and-one, two...' and so on. Now you have a leisurely pace, every so often interrupted by a burst of activity. Why? Perhaps you are rushing between people with your tray and then serving them slowly, or the other way round, or perhaps you keep dropping things or falling over. Try the same changes of rhythm with other actions as in the previous exercise.

Some everyday actions have a regular rhythm—such as walking, sawing wood, or kneading dough—but most are more complex and have an irregular, changing rhythm. The Tempo-rhythm still exists, though, and can still be changed to transform the scene. There may also be more than one rhythm at work at the same time; perhaps a teenage boy is lying on the sofa trying to watch television while his mother is frantically tidying up and trying to get him to get ready before a guest arrives. Stanislavski also distinguished between Outer Tempo-rhythm, relating to the body and voice, and Inner Tempo-rhythm, that of the mind and emotions. In many cases these will be the same, but sometimes there may be a sharp contrast between the two. For instance, somebody being interviewed for a job they really want may be projecting a calm, relaxed outward appearance but be nervous and tense inside. Or a circus acrobat may perform some amazingly elaborate movements while remaining calm and focused inside.

Drama from music

Find a piece of music without words, preferably with plenty of changes in tempo and rhythm. Working individually or in small groups, listen to what actions the music suggests to you at each point and build up a whole scene that fits to the music. Listen also for conflicting rhythms over the top of one another and think about how they affect the action in your scene.

The exercises in this section have mostly been to create or modify a scene based on a given Tempo-rhythm. In practice, the process is likely to work the other way round.

Tempo-rhythm in rehearsal

Take a scene from a play you are rehearsing or studying. Work out the Inner and Outer Tempo-rhythms of each character at every point in the scene, experimenting with different Tempo-rhythms until you obtain the effect you want. Write out the action of the scene like a music score to remind you.

Speech Tempo-rhythm

Spoken words also have a Tempo-rhythm; this is most obvious when speaking verse, but it also applies to prose. Pauses are as important a part of the Tempo-rhythm of dialogue as the words. There may be variations depending on mood, circumstances and what is being said, and a character may also have a general Speech Tempo-rhythm influenced by personality, age, accent and so on. You may even find similarities in the Tempo-rhythm of a whole play's dialogue, or even in all the works of a particular playwright.

The 'System' in Rehearsal

Stanislavski's students at his Studio began working on plays towards the end of their second year and did not put together a full production until their fourth year. They were taught a technique known as the Method of Physical Action (or the Method of Analysis Through Physical Action) in which the staging of a play evolved organically from experimental work during rehearsals rather than being presented to the actors by the director for them to learn and copy. The students wrote all of their discoveries during rehearsals in their personal notebooks, not so that they could be marked or graded but to focus their thoughts and to remind them of ideas that have come from their work. Rehearsals could go on for a year or more, and so some kind of memory aide was necessary.

Although Stanislavski preferred to use everyday terms to make it easier for his students to understand and remember them, the most famous English translations are those in *An Actor Prepares*: Superobjective, Objective, Unit and Through Line of Action. In the Russian version, *An Actor's Work On Himself*, the terms used are Supertask, Task, Bit and Through-Action (in America, the word Beat is sometimes used due to a misunderstanding of Russian teachers talking about Bits). At the Studio, he referred to Supertask, Task, Episodes (Facts are smaller Episodes, and he sometimes referred to both as Events) and Through-Action, and these are the terms used here.

Using the Method of Physical Actions in rehearsal
The following section describes the major elements of the Method of Physical Actions and how they can be used in rehearsal. The best way of understanding these

methods is to go through them with a text that you intend to perform. It is a lengthy process and should not be rushed if it is to be effective.

Preliminary analysis

Read through the play several times to thoroughly absorb everything that happens. Summarise the action in half a page. This should give the basic structure of the play and a sequence of the major events. Take each of the main parts of the play and examine the **Given Circumstances**, thinking about what you would do **If** this happened to you, now. Improvise these sections from the Given Circumstances, not making any attempt to learn the scripted dialogue at this stage. Create and improvise the **Before-time**—everything that happens to the characters that the playwright hasn't written before they enter the scene—and the **After-time**—what will happen after the scene ends. Now create a more detailed summary of the play from your Given Circumstances.

Supertask

At this stage, you should create a provisional **Supertask**. This is the main theme or objective of the play, the reason it was written and the task that all the scenes are working towards. This is the backbone of all of your work on the play and will define the whole approach to the production. However, as you work further on the play you may find a better Supertask and decide to change it, reworking any scenes that are affected by the change. For example, Stanislavski defined the Supertask of Chekhov's *Three Sisters* as 'The desire for fulfilment, to live a full life.' For his 1911 production of *Hamlet* with Gordon Craig, he settled on 'Discovering the meaning of existence', which defines their particular approach to the play but which would not be at all appropriate for most other productions of this play.

Through-action and Counter-through-action

Next, create the **Through-action** for your character. This is the overall action that your character is trying to perform throughout the play, the goal that each individual action in the play is working towards. For instance, Romeo's goal may be to take Juliet to where they can always be together. The **Counter-through-action** is whatever is preventing your character from immediately achieving this goal, such as the deadly feud between the Montagues and the Capulets.

Breaking down the play

Episodes, Basic Actions, Tasks, Facts

Divide the play up into **Episodes**. These are the main sections of the play, each with its own logical sequence of events. These may or may not correspond to scene or act divisions in the script. You should only use as many Episodes as you need to represent the major events in the play.

For each Episode, define your character's **Basic Action**. This is what your character is trying to accomplish during this Episode. Think about what you would do 'If' you were in the same situation.

Break each Episode down into **Facts**—a logical sequence of events that together describe the action of the Episode.

For each Fact, define your character's **Task**—what they are trying to achieve—and create a sequence of **Actions** that will get them there.

Note that Basic Actions, Tasks and Actions are unique to each character, whereas each actor must be working to the same agreed Episodes and Facts.

Work on improvised versions of each Fact, refining them so that the Task is achieved logically but any unnecessary action is stripped away.

Subtext

The **Subtext** is the part of the play that happens in the characters' minds but which they do not say or do. A major part of this is the **Inner Monologue**, the thoughts running through the character's mind throughout the scene. What do they think when someone is speaking to them, or when they are speaking to someone else, or when they are just in the background? **Mental Images** are the pictures that the character has in his or her head at each moment. Create the Inner Monologue for your character for each Fact, and decide what Mental Images they have.

The text

Up to now, all dialogue and moves have been improvised. Now it is time to join this work up with the words of the text. Read the play as a group for the first time. Read it through a few times, making more notes each time on anything that strikes you as significant. Also note down any difficult words that you need to look up or any historical or social references that you need to research in order to properly understand what happens in the play. At this point, the actors begin to learn their lines.

Go through the whole play, Fact by Fact, with the actors speaking their lines and explaining their Subtext. Work on external characterisation: how your character looks and walks, any characteristic gestures they have.

Preparing the production

Fix the moves for each Fact based on the work you have done so far. Keep the Subtext in your head while you are rehearsing the scenes. Find the correct Tempo-rhythm for each scene.

Go back to the earliest work you did on the production. Make sure that the Through-action and the Counter-through-action for your character is clear and that all of your Basic Actions contribute towards it. As a group, look at the Supertask you originally defined. If it is still appropriate, check that your work on the play contribute towards this Supertask. If your subsequent discoveries lead you to believe that the Supertask is not correct for your production, redefine it.

Sample Questions

1. Demonstrate the workings of Stanislavski's Method of Physical Actions as a rehearsal method. Use your experience of rehearsing for one particular production as an example.
2. Stanislavski was keen to demonstrate that his 'system' was not only appropriate for naturalistic styles of acting. To what extent is this true? What elements of the 'system' may conflict with non-naturalistic styles of performance?

2 Edward Gordon Craig

Biography Overview

Craig was born in 1872 in Stevenage in Hertfordshire, England; his father was the architect Edward William Godwin (himself a noted theatre director and designer) and his mother, Ellen Terry, was the principal actress of the great actor-manager Sir Henry Irving's theatre company. Edward and his actress sister Edith used the name Craig as a stage name after Edith saw the island Ailsa Craig off the west coast of Scotland when she was fifteen, but he only officially became Edward Henry Gordon Craig (named after his father Edward Godwin, his godfather Henry Irving and his godmother Lady Gordon) when he registered the name by Deed Poll in 1893. His mother and father, who were never married, parted when he was three and his mother married Charles Wardell (stage name Charles Kelly) but the marriage did not last. Wardell, separated from Terry by this time, died in 1885 and Craig's real father Godwin died the year after.

Craig first appeared on stage at the age of six, and he played his first speaking role, as a gardener's boy, at the age of thirteen, when his mother was on tour with Irving's company. In 1889, he became a member of Irving's company at the Lyceum, and played a number of major roles, including Hamlet and Romeo, for this and other companies over the next few years. In 1897, he gave up acting and instead designed bookplates, and created drawings and woodcuts, many of which were printed in the magazine *The Page*, which he edited from 1898 to 1901.

He began directing with a charity performance of De Musset's *No Trifling with Love* in 1893, but his most important work as a director and designer started with the production of Purcell's *Dido and Aeneas* in 1900 for the newly formed Purcell Operatic Society with musical direction by Martin

Shaw. The cast of seventy, with the exception of the two title roles, consisted entirely of amateur performers, and rehearsals went on for seven months for a performance at the Hampstead Conservatoire of Music. Craig created a false proscenium for the production, which concealed an electric lighting system that was without precedent. He used coloured light projected through gauze onto cloths to create effects very different from the painted backcloths used in nearly all theatre productions at the time. Unfortunately, despite its great success, the production made a loss and Craig and Shaw earned no money for their seven months' work. They worked together again on Purcell's *The Masque of Love* for a production at the Coronet Theatre, Notting Hill Gate in 1901, which made a profit, and again on Handel's *Acis and Galatea* at the Great Queen Street Theatre in 1902, which left a number of debts that Ellen Terry had to satisfy. All of these operas had very simple plots and the visual effects were achieved using costumes, fabrics, lighting and stylised movements from the performers. In December 1902, Craig staged his last production with amateur performers, Laurence Housman's play *Bethlehem*, in the Great Hall of the Imperial Institute in South Kensington with incidental music by Martin Shaw.

At the age of thirty, Craig decided it was time for him to earn a proper living in the theatre instead of depending on his mother's generosity. His mother had left Irving to set up her own company at the Imperial Theatre in Westminster, and Craig persuaded her to open with Ibsen's *The Vikings at Helgeland*, which he was to direct and design. For the first time, Craig had to deal with the world of professional theatre, and many of his ideas were questioned or objected to for practical, financial or artistic reasons. The business manager questioned every expense and the actors questioned why the play had to be interpreted rather than simply following stage directions. Craig was not prepared to compromise his vision for any reason, and clashes were inevitable. Despite some critical praise for the visual spectacle of the production when it opened in April 1903, audiences did not come, and Terry closed the production after three weeks. It was replaced with

Much Ado About Nothing after just two weeks of rehearsal, again with a design by her son but with a much simpler—and cheaper—construction. Even this was not enough to recoup the losses, and Terry had to take the company on tour.

Craig clashed with the professional theatre once again when he was asked by Otto Brahm to create designs for Otway's *Venice Preserved* at the Lessing Theatre, Berlin in 1905. Brahm wanted realistic scene designs, but Craig wanted to rebuild the stage; in the end only two of Craig's designs were used after extensive modifications. He decided to promote his ideas by writing and by exhibiting his designs around the world, especially in Germany and London. His book, *The Art of the Theatre* was published in 1905 in German and then in English, and it was re-released with further essays in 1911 as *On The Art of the Theatre*.

In December 1904, Craig saw the great dancer Isadora Duncan perform in Berlin. They began a two-year affair that produced two children, but they were also united by a belief that movement is the fundamental component of drama. Duncan introduced Craig to the Italian actress Eleonora Duse for him to design a production of Ibsen's *Rosmersholm* to be produced in Florence. On the strength of the triumphant opening performance, Duse wished for their collaboration to continue, but it was terminated the following February when she considered that Craig's furious response to the stage manager in Nice (who sawed two feet from the bottom of the set to accommodate the lower proscenium opening) was excessive. Craig settled in Florence for the next nine years and took out a lease on a small open-air theatre called the Arena Goldoni, which he used as an office and workshop and was to be the site of his School for the Art of the Theatre until the outbreak of the First World War in 1914 cut short his plans. His magazine *The Mask*, for which he wrote most of the articles under a variety of different names, was launched in 1908 and continued, apart from a break for the war, until 1929.

He created a great deal of written work, drawings and research in Florence, but did not direct or design any productions because of the impossible conditions he laid down each time he received an offer, with one exception. Isadora Duncan told Stanislavski about Craig and showed him some of Craig's work while she was on tour in Russia in 1908, and Stanislavski invited Craig to spend a month with the Moscow Art Theatre to see their work. They agreed to collaborate on a production of *Hamlet* with Stanislavski as director and Craig as set and costume designer. Stanislavski began rehearsals early the following year in a mostly realistic style, but when Craig came back in April 1909 with his ideas and sketches it was announced that Craig was to both direct and design. His design used tall screens, moved in full view of the audience to transform the stage from one shape to another without the need for lengthy scene changes in blackout. Craig began to fall out with the actors and the management again, and after a year's break in rehearsals due to Stanislavski's illness with typhoid fever Craig lost interest in the project. Stanislavski began to have doubts about Craig's ideas and took over the direction, but when Craig returned for the first run-through he caused such a disturbance that he was told to stay away until the final dress rehearsals. An hour before the curtain rose on the first night in January 1912, one of the screens fell over and knocked all of the others down, so there had to be lengthy blackouts for scene changes after all. The production was still a success, although some critics noticed the discrepancy between Craig's stylised staging and design and Stanislavski's actors' realistic acting. The scenes closest to Craig's original intentions created a great impression, and his screens, despite their disastrous failure on this occasion, were very influential and were adopted by others.

In 1908, Craig published an essay in *The Mask* entitled 'The actor and the Über-Marionette', which seemed to call for the actor to be replaced by some kind of puppet for the director to manipulate. He wrote in the preface to the second edition of *On the Art of the Theatre* in 1924, 'The Über-Marionette is the actor plus fire, minus egoism, the fire of the gods and demons, without the smoke and steam of mortality.'

After the First World War, his only production of note was Ibsen's *The Pretenders* at the Royal Theatre Copenhagen in 1926. By the start of the Second World War he had settled in France, where he remained until his death at the age of ninety-four in 1966.

Theory and Practice

A question of style

Craig was brought up in the theatre and worked in it as an actor from an early age. When he criticised contemporary theatre, he was speaking as someone with a thorough knowledge and great love of the theatre and believed he could transform it into something infinitely greater than anything offered at the time.

In his essay *Rearrangements*, written in 1915, Craig examined eight areas of the theatrical presentation: mode of speech (verse or prose), the actor's delivery of speech, scenery, actors, movement, light, make-up and facial expression. His conclusion was that in the current theatre, 'the words, actors, their speech and facial expressions are organic … the scenes and the disguised faces [make-up] are inorganic … the light and movement are half one thing and half the other'. He believed this clash of the naturalistic and the obviously artificial to be inartistic, and proposed two different ways of rearranging the same elements. The first moves away from any naturalistic form of presentation in all of the elements:

The poet's work to be as it is—an unnatural mode of speech or verse.

The actor's work to be an unnatural mode of delivery.

The scene to be a non-natural invention, timeless, and of no locality.

Actors to be disguised beyond recognition, like the marionette.

Movements conventionalised according to some other system.

Light frankly non-natural, disposed so as to illuminate scene and actors.

Masks.

Expression to be dependent on the masks and the conventional movements, both of which are dependent on the skill of the actor.

He also proposed a similar list for a realistic approach:

The poet's work to be written in a colloquial mode of speech, natural—as improvisation is.

The actor's delivery to be colloquial.

The scene to be a facsimile or photographic reproduction of nature, even to the use of real trees, real earth, bricks, etc.

The actors in no way disguised, but selected according to their likeness to the part which is to be acted.

Movements as natural as the speech.

The light of day or night.

The faces of the actors paintless.

The expression as natural as the movements or speech.

Craig believed that a production must have a consistent approach, and that it makes no sense, for instance, to put natural acting in front of a painted backdrop or to try to speak poetic drama in a natural, colloquial way. He wrote, 'to mix the real and the unreal, the genuine and the sham—*when you are not forced to do so*—is at all times, whether in life or in art, an error, a misconception of the nature of all things, a parody of purpose'. Of the two approaches, he favoured the first because he claimed, 'for ages and not merely centuries, all art experts— that is to say, artists and art theorists too—have decided that, no matter what the work is to be, if it is to be called an art work it must be made solely from *inorganic* material'.

Finding the organic and the inorganic
Think about a stage production you have seen recently or have been involved with. Think about the style of the elements of the production described by Craig:

Is the dialogue written like natural speech or is it more poetic?

Do the actors speak the dialogue like natural speech or in a stylised way?

Is the scenery designed to look like a real place or is it more symbolic?

Are the actors using their own natural appearance or are they disguised as a character?

Do the actors move in a natural way or a stylised, dance-like way?

Is the lighting designed to copy how natural light would fall or is it designed for effects?

Do the actors use make-up or masks or their natural faces?

Do the actors use natural or stylised facial expressions?

Each of these may fall between the two extremes mentioned above or may be different from one scene to the next or for different characters. Do you believe Craig would have seen a consistency in style in this production? Does it tend towards being organic (more naturalistic) or inorganic (more symbolic)? Think about how you could change each of the eight elements in order to make the production (i) more organic; (ii) more inorganic. Try to stage your own version of a short section of the play in these two different ways.

To Craig, this consistency of style was absolutely fundamental to the sort of theatre he wished to create. Where his productions failed, it was usually as a result of compromises he was forced to make when he was collaborating with others, such as where his symbolic designs for *Hamlet* clashed with the psychological realism of Stanislavski's actors. Isadora Duncan said of Eleonora Duse in Craig's production of *Rosmersholm* in 1906, 'With her unerring genius she adapted herself to every great line and to each shaft of light which enveloped her.' However, 'But when the other actors came on—Rosmer, for instance, who put his hands in his pockets—they seemed to be like stage hands who had walked on by mistake. It was positively painful.' Great actors were able to adapt their style of performance to suit the style of the production; others looked out of place.

The stage director

Craig's vision of theatre depends very strongly on having a single person with a complete vision and absolute control over every aspect of the production, variously referred to by Craig as 'stage manager', 'stage director', 'master of the drama', '*regisseur*' and '*metteur-en-scène*'. The role of a director as a specific job in the theatre was still a relatively new one—although this function had always been carried out by someone, such as the lead actor or the playwright— and the title 'director' was not yet settled on. In *The Art of the Theatre: The First Dialogue*, written by Craig in 1905 in the form of a scripted conversation between a 'stage director' and a 'playgoer', the director asks,

> A has written a play which B promises to interpret faithfully. In so delicate a matter as the interpretation of so elusive a thing as the spirit of a play, which, do you think, will be the surest way to preserve the unity of that spirit? Will it be best if B does all the work himself? or will it do to give the work into the hands of C, D and E, each of whom see or think differently to B or A?

In other words, should one person be in charge of the artistic vision of the whole production, or should the stage director, designer, lighting designer, sound designer and actors all be allowed to come up with their own vision for their particular role? Of course Craig's question is heavily loaded towards the first option. The playgoer later asks whether this means that the director paints all the scenery and cuts and sews all the costumes, to which the director answers,

> No, I will not say that he does so in every case and for every play, but he must have done so at one time or another during his apprenticeship, or must have closely studied all the technical points of these complicated

crafts. Then will he be able to guide the skilled craftsmen in their different departments.

A director need not be a technical expert or a skilled craftsman in every department as long as other people exist in the company who can carry out his ideas, but he should have an intimate knowledge of everything that can be done in each department.

Within this dialogue, Craig breaks down the tasks of a director chronologically:

Read the play for the first time to find 'the whole colour, rhythm, action of the thing'.

Put the play aside and examine first impressions of the play. Craig places particular emphasis on the colours that are conjured up in the director's mind by this first reading.

Give the play a second reading to test these first impressions and make notes of ideas.

It may take a dozen readings before the director has solid ideas for how scenes should look, including scenery, costumes and actors. He should ignore any stage directions in the script and should not think about historical accuracy, realism or prettiness. He begins by choosing 'certain colours which seem to be in harmony with the spirit of the play, rejecting other colours as out of tune'.

The director adds major objects that will be featured in the design: 'an arch, a fountain, a balcony, a bed'.

To this, he adds any objects mentioned in the script that must be visible. Craig did not believe in adding objects purely for aesthetic reasons, or cluttering up the stage with unnecessary objects that may divert the audience's attention away from the action.

At this point, he adds the actors to the picture. Remember that this is still the planning and design stage, long before rehearsals begin. The director 'adds, one by one, each character which appears in the play, and gradually each movement of each character, and each costume'. In Craig's system, every movement and position of every actor is designed by the director in advance and taught to the actor. He talks about 'patterns' and advises the director that if a mistake is found in the pattern, the design must be 'unpicked', working backwards, even if it means starting all over again.

The designs are handed to the craftsmen to create scenery and costumes as specified by the director.

Once the construction is underway, actors are allocated parts, and must learn their lines before the first rehearsal.

When the scenery is set and the actors are costumed, the director places the actors in position and commences lighting the scene.

The next stage is 'the manipulation of the figures in all their movements and speeches'—in other words, teaching the actors every move and way of speaking that the director has worked out in advance for them to reproduce precisely.

Craig's stage director

Look at Act III scene 1 of Shakespeare's *A Midsummer Night's Dream*; this scene involves human and fairy characters as well as magical transformation. Go through Craig's process described above to create your own production of just this scene (it will help if you know the whole play). To do this properly, you must work out every small detail of the design, sound effects, music, the actors' movements and the way the lines should be spoken. If your time is limited, you may wish to focus on a section of the scene for the finer details, but make sure you have worked out how this section fits into the whole scene. You will probably be unable to have your scenery and costumes made, so make detailed notes and sketches of your ideas. If possible, stage some or all of the scene with actors, making sure they reproduce your detailed instructions precisely without any improvisations or deviations from your plan.

Craig and the actor

Craig has often been portrayed as someone who despises actors and would like them replaced by puppets; like most myths, there is a grain of truth in this but it has been greatly distorted. He clashed many times with actors when directing his own productions, but then he was asking them to work in ways that were completely contrary to how they had been always been used to working and he was not prepared to compromise his vision for any reason. Every person on the production's team, including every actor, had to follow the director's instructions precisely, but in order to do this, they all had to be intelligent and talented in their particular field.

While Craig did have problems working with actors in general, he greatly admired some actors, such as Eleonora Duse and his godfather, Henry Irving. He published a biography of Irving in 1930, and said of him,

> From the first to the last moment that Irving stood on the stage each moment was significant ... every sound, each movement, was intentional—clear-cut, measured dance: nothing real—all massively artificial—yet all flashing with the light and the pulse of nature. A fine style.

To Craig, describing an actor's work as 'massively artificial' was a great compliment. He agreed with his mother's view that acting cannot be taught because it depends on instinct and accident. To Craig, this meant that acting is not an art and therefore actors are not artists, because he believed that art is something deliberate, carefully planned and artificial. In his famous 1907 essay *The Actor and The Über-marionette*, he begins by stating firmly that he has no wish to join in illogical attacks on actors and acting that are sometimes made by 'literary or private gentlemen ... On the strength of having gone to see plays all their lives, or on the strength of never having gone to see a play in their lives.' Instead he carefully lays down what he refers to as 'the logical facts of a curious case':

> Acting is not an art. It is therefore incorrect to speak of the actor as an artist. For accident is the enemy of the artist. Art is the exact antithesis of pandemonium, and pandemonium is created by the tumbling together of many accidents. Art only arrives by design ... the mind of the actor, we see, is less powerful than his emotion,

for emotion is able to win over the mind to assist in the destruction of that which the mind would produce; and as the mind becomes the slave of emotion it follows that accident upon accident must be continually occurring.

A painter or a playwright may create a piece of art that expresses a great deal of emotion, but this is achieved through careful planning and calculation and not, as with an actor, by inducing the emotion in himself. In a slightly later essay the following year entitled *The Artists of the Theatre of the Future*, Craig said he did not believe Shakespeare to have written *Othello* when he was in a fit of jealousy, writing the first words that came to mind whilst he was consumed by passion; instead he believed 'that the words had to pass through our author's head and that it was just through the quality of his imagination and the strength of his brain that the richness of his nature was able to be entirely and clearly expressed'.

He wrote in the earlier essay, 'The actor must go, and in his place comes the inanimate figure—the Über-marionette we may call him, until he has won for himself a better name.' He believed the marionette or puppet had been debased as simply an amusement for children, 'a rather superior doll', and 'All puppets are now but low comedians' but even these figures contain some of the attributes he desires from his actors:

The applause may thunder or dribble, their hearts beat no faster, no slower, their signals do not grow hurried or confused; and, though drenched in a torrent of bouquets and love, the face of the leading lady remains as solemn, as beautiful and as remote as ever. There is something more than a flash of genius in the marionette, and there is something in him more than the flashiness of displayed personality.

The puppet is not affected by emotion, will not be influenced by the reactions of the audience and will not display parts of his or her own personality alongside that of the character. However Craig did not want to replace actors with puppets; instead he wanted to create a new type of actor who would take on the aspects of the marionette that he wanted but go beyond this: 'The Über-marionette will not compete with life—rather it will go beyond it. Its ideal will not be the flesh and blood but rather the body in a trance—it will aim to clothe itself with a death-like beauty while exhaling a living spirit.'

Craig's ideal actor, therefore, is not a carved wooden puppet but an intelligent human being who uses skill and reason, not emotion or improvisation, to create a performance in a style that is in harmony with every other component of the production, from the design to the music. The actor is never carried away with the emotion of the role he is playing, always remaining coolly aloof from the character and in total control of his performance. The style of the actor's performance, like the style of the production as a whole, should not be an attempt to copy real life; instead, his movement, speech, costume and make-up or mask should blend in with the rest of the production.

Craig's actor

Look at your plan for *A Midsummer Night's Dream* from the last exercise. If you staged the scene or a part of it, did your actors' performances fit in with the style of the rest of the production? Look at each element of the actor's performance—such as voice, movement, facial expression, make-up or mask, costume—and examine how you could tailor the performances of the actors to fit in better with your overall plan for the production.

Look at the following characters and come up with a design for their movement, make-up or mask, speech, costume and so on. You will need to create an overall style for the play, as the characters must fit into a particular production rather than standing alone.

    Shakespeare's *Hamlet*
    Ibsen's Nora from *A Doll's* House
    Arthur Miller's Willy Loman from *Death of a Salesman*
    Brecht's *Mother Courage*

Stage design

Although Craig was an actor and a director, at heart he was a designer, and in every production he worked on, each element on stage, including the actors, was carefully arranged with the eye of a painter or sculptor. Unlike painting or sculpture, his creations moved in four dimensions, and the stage picture had to work at every moment even though it was constantly changing. Many of Craig's designs were not for a specific production but to illustrate his ideas about a particular play or for a different use of light, colour, scenery or arrangement of figures on the stage. Many of his designs have a similar style: small human figures against a light, plain background; high vertical lines using high walls, huge archways and massive pillars; monochrome images that create specific moods using light and shadow. Craig said, 'Remember that on a sheet of paper which is but two inches square you can make a line which seems to tower miles in the air, and you can do the same on your stage, for it is all a matter of proportion.' Those who criticised Craig's designs as impractical—in some of his drawings, the size of the human figure implies that the scenery is around sixty feet high—missed the fact that these were illustrations of ideas and not completed designs to put on stage.

The Steps

In 1905, Craig created a series of four drawings with accompanying texts called *The Steps*. He wrote that there are two kinds of drama, 'the drama of speech and the drama of silence'. The latter includes 'dramas where speech becomes paltry and inadequate', and he uses as an example the work of the symbolist playwright Maeterlinck, who 'leads us up to a fountain or into a wood, or brings a stream upon us, makes a cock crow, and shows us how dramatic these things are'. As well as the natural world, the man-made world can also create a drama of silence, in particular 'that noblest of all men's work, architecture'. He wrote:

> There is something so human and so poignant to me in a great city at a time of the night when there are no people

about and no sounds. It is dreadfully sad until you walk till six o'clock in the morning. Then it is very exciting.

As the title suggests, this work focuses on one specific architectural feature that he found particularly fascinating: steps. He used the same basic flight of steps, bordered on both sides by high walls, to create four moods, which differed from one another by the lighting and shadow, the arrangement of figures on the steps and the features at the top and bottom.

The steps

Draw a wide set of steps as though you were facing them with a high wall on either side. Make four copies of this basic drawing. One at a time, add figures to the drawing (men, women, children, animals) in a way that implies action, that they are doing something. Add shading, and perhaps colour, to show the mood of the scene. There may be other objects at the top and bottom, and these do not have to be the same in each drawing. This is not an exercise in drawing, so the aim is not to create the best-looking pictures. Try to make the mood of the scene and the positions of the figures clear, adding explanatory notes (just as Craig did) if necessary to clarify what is happening.

Craig's four moods show:

The mood—and the shading in the picture—is light as three children play on the steps.

Many children dance about at the top of the steps, whilst at the bottom, 'I have made the earth respond to their movements. The earth is made to dance.'

A man walks around a maze drawn on the floor at the bottom of the steps, and a woman walks down the steps, apparently towards him.

This dark image shows a single figure, slumped against the wall, halfway down the steps. Craig's explanation adds to the story of the picture. The unhappy figure emerges from the shadows and slumps into the position in the picture. Then a fountain at the top of the steps begins slowly to rise higher and higher, and is then joined by a second fountain next to it. Once the fountains have reached their highest point, a light appears at the bottom of the steps as though through a window with the shadows of a man and a woman in it. 'The figure on the steps raises his head. The drama is finished.'

Screens

In his 1923 book *Scene*, Craig described and explained his philosophy for creating scenery at that time. He believed that any building from any era could be represented on stage by an arrangement of simple, flat walls. These are arranged in a way that gives an impression of the place that the stage represents without adding the surface detail, decoration or ornamentation, as 'The artist is to speak to spectators through scene, he is not to display a large doll's house for them.' The scenery is white so it can be coloured with light, 'for it can be shaded to any tone of grey, blackened by shade; coloured any colour, and that without changing the colour of the actors face, hands, or figure'. The walls are plain as 'You can see a face—a hand—a vase—a statue better when it is backed by a flat plain non-coloured surface than when backed by something on which a coloured pattern or some other object is painted or carved.' The actor therefore appears as a bas-relief figure against a plain surface, with different sets of lighting instruments lighting actor and scenery so that one can be changed in colour and intensity without affecting the other. To Craig, controlled lighting was one of the most important new tools to the stage designer and not simply a method of illuminating the stage.

To facilitate this style of design, Craig patented a system of movable screens, which allowed any theatre to completely change the configuration of its stage area from one performance to the next or even during a performance. His 1915 essay *The Thousand Scenes in One Scene* reads like a sales brochure, and it goes into such detailed description that it challenges those of his detractors who claimed that his ideas were impractical. A scene would be made up of at least four and as many as twelve of these screens, arranged to give an impression of the place being represented. All screens are of the same height but different widths for flexibility— 'With screens of narrow dimensions curved forms are produced, for larger rectangular spaces broader leaved screens are used, and for varied and broken forms all sizes are employed'—and can be made from wood or from canvas stretched over a wooden frame. They are self-supporting, so they can be moved quickly from one location to another. Each screen is made up of a number of 'leaves', between two and ten, hinged to fold both ways. They are monochrome to give the actors a light background to work against and to allow colour and shade to be controlled with lighting. He acknowledged that other scenic elements could be added to his screens, but warned against excess:

> Sometimes certain additions may be made to this scene, such as a flight of steps, a window, a bridge, a balcony, and of course the necessary furniture, though great care and reserve must be exercised in making these additions so as to avoid the ridiculous.

The screens for Craig and Stanislavski's production of *Hamlet* at the Moscow Art Theatre in 1912 were not very successful, but others had already adopted the idea and it continued to influence directors and designers. The Irish poet and playwright W B Yeats used Craig's screens for his play *The Hour Glass* at the Abbey Theatre in Dublin as early as 1910, commenting that 'henceforth I shall be able, by means so simple that one laughs, to lay the events of my plays amid a grandeur like that of Babylon … he has banished a whole world that wearied me and was undignified and given me forms and lights upon which I can play as upon some stringed instrument'.

Screens
Cut out a figure of a person from card of about seventy-five millimetres or three inches in height. Stick it to a base to make it freestanding. Create some model screens, similar

to the ones described by Craig, also out of card (use white card for this; you can colour the human model for contrast). Each should be the same height (three or four times the height of your person) but you should create a variety of different widths. Fold the card screens lengthwise at least once so that each consists of a number of "leaves" that can be folded either way to change the screen's shape (this will also make them freestanding). Experiment with arranging these screens in different ways to create a scene that suggests each of the following. How could you use coloured light, white light and shadow to create mood? Do you need any other scenic items (staircases, archways, fountains, pillars, furniture) to complete the scene? Your stage set should give the impression of the location, not recreate it in all its naturalistic details, and too much extra scenery will stop the fluid changes of location that the screens are supposed to allow.

Macbeth's castle and the blasted heath from *Macbeth*

The Hall of the Mountain King from Ibsen's *Peer Gynt*

The street, the masked ball, Juliet's bedroom and Friar Lawrence's cell from *Romeo and Juliet*

Sample Questions

1. How does Craig's process for creating a production of a play differ from Stanislavski's?
2. How can Craig's screens be used to create different locations and moods on stage? Show how they could be used for a production of any play you know well that has scenes in different locations.
3. How can lighting (light, shade and colour) be used to create and change mood and location on stage? Relate your answer to Craig's ideas.

3 **Antonin Artaud**

Biography Overview

Antoine Marie Joseph Artaud (Antonin is a diminutive of Antoine) was born in Marseille on 4 September 1896 to a wealthy shipping agent and his wife. At the age of five he became seriously ill and was diagnosed with meningitis, which is sometimes blamed for his later problems, but this may not have been meningitis as we know it today and his psychological problems appear to have begun much later. At the age of nineteen, he spent some time in a sanatorium for nervous disorders at Rouguières near Marseille. When he left, he was called up into the army, but after spending nine months at a military training camp at Digne he was released on medical grounds.

For the next few years, Artaud spent time in a number of sanatoria and started to take laudanum, beginning a battle with drug dependency that was to last the rest of his life. In 1920, he moved to Paris and lodged with Dr Edouard Toulouse, head psychiatrist at the asylum at Villejuif and founder of the literary periodical *Demain*. At first, Toulouse gave Artaud light work, but after a while he left him to run *Demain* in which he published a number of his own poems and articles. Artaud met some major figures of Parisian artistic society, including the director of the Théâtre de l'Oeuvre, Aurélien Lugné-Poe, and on 17 February 1921, Artaud made his first appearance as an actor at Lugné-Poe's theatre. Later that year, he joined the Atelier, a workshop of actors led by Charles Dullin who was one of the first proponents of a total theatre in which movement, gesture, mime and sound are at least as important as words. Artaud, as actor, set designer and costume designer, was involved with a number of productions toured by the Atelier in 1922. After Dullin expressed concern at his strange interpretation of some roles, Artaud left to join Georges Pitoeff's company at the Comédie des Champs-Elysées. Artaud continued to write and have his work published. In 1923, Jacques Rivière, editor of the *Nouvelle Revue Française*, rejected some of his poems, but they wrote a number of letters to one another, which were published in the *NRF* and later as a book.

After his father died in 1924 Artaud was no longer financially supported, so he began acting in films to earn an income. He also became involved in the Surrealist movement, and the following year he became director of the Surrealiste Bureau de Recherches. He edited the third edition of *La Révolution Surréaliste*, in which he published open letters to the heads of institutions that the Surrealists opposed: the Pope, the Dalai Lama, the Schools of Buddha, head doctors of asylums and rectors of European universities.

In 1926, Artaud collaborated with playwright Roger Vitrac to create the Théâtre Alfred Jarry, named after a controversial playwright that they both admired. The November issue of *NRF* published the *First Manifesto of the Théâtre Alfred Jarry*, which contained the seeds of his later ideas for the Theatre of Cruelty. The Surrealists were critical of Artaud's ventures, accusing him of commercialism for setting up his own theatre and for acting in films. Artaud disagreed strongly with the Surrealists' decision to join the Communist party. The Surrealists formally expelled Artaud in November 1926.

In 1927 he played two of his most famous film roles, Marat in Abel Gance's *Napoléon* and the friar in Carl Dreyer's *La Passion de Jeanne d'Arc*, and his own script, *The Seashell and the Clergyman*, was filmed by Germaine Dulac. At the time Artaud loudly proclaimed his dissatisfaction with this last film, but years later when films such as Buñuel's *Un Chien Andalou* and Cocteau's *The Blood Of A Poet* were hailed as classics of Surrealist cinema, he claimed that these other films merely followed his lead. The last performance of the Théâtre Alfred Jarry was in January 1929, but Artaud continued to act in films, including, in 1930, the French version of GW Pabst's film of Brecht's *Threepenny Opera*.

Artaud saw a display of Balinese dancing in 1931 that he believed realised many of his ideas on theatre. His article on Balinese theatre, published in *NRF*, began a series of articles and lectures which later formed the heart of his most famous book of essays, *The Theatre and its Double*. *The First Manifesto of the Theatre of Cruelty* was published in October 1932 in the *NRF*. He adapted Seneca's *Atreus and Thyestes*, wrote a scenario for *Conquest of Mexico*, worked on a play based on Shelly's *The Cenci*, completed his book *Heliogabalus* and wrote the *Second Manifesto of the Theatre of Cruelty* over the next couple of years. *The Cenci* opened in May 1935 at the Théâtre des Folies-Wagram, but it was both a critical and a box office failure and closed after seventeen performances. Artaud took this failure badly, believing, correctly, that it signalled the end of his career in theatre writing and directing.

In 1936, Artaud went to Mexico to study the culture of the tribal Indians. While he was there he experienced the hallucinogenic drug peyotl used in tribal ceremonies. The following year he became engaged to be married to Cécile Schramme and had treatment for his drug addictions, but neither was to last long. By this time he was fascinated by magic and mysticism and was convinced that a sword he had obtained in Havana had magical powers and that a walking stick he had been given by a friend had once belonged to St Patrick. In 1937, he travelled to Ireland to return St Patrick's cane to its homeland.

The events of September 1937 in Dublin are unclear, but they resulted in Artaud being detained by the police and put onto the SS Washington bound for Le Havre, and his cane was lost. Whilst on this ship, Artaud attacked a steward and a mechanic whom he believed were trying to harm him, but he was overpowered and put into a straitjacket. On arrival in Le Havre, he was handed over to the French authorities who imprisoned him in an asylum.

As Artaud was moved between asylums, his friends campaigned for his release but he had been imprisoned for six years before they managed to have him transferred to a rural institution at Rodez, outside the area of France occupied by the Germans, in the care of psychiatrist Gaston Férdière in 1943. Férdière, who knew and respected Artaud as a poet, treated him as a friend and gave him his own room. Although he continued to behave strangely and to fantasise, he carried out some translation work and wrote further essays about his trip to Mexico. Férdière began to use a new form of treatment on Artaud, electric shock therapy, which Artaud found extremely traumatic.

Artaud's friends and supporters continued to campaign for his release. In 1946, after Artaud had been incarcerated for nine years in various institutions, Férdière agreed to his release provided that he was financially supported. A committee was formed, and artists and writers including Picasso, Duchamp, Giacommetti, Braque and Sartre donated work for auction. A benefit performance at the Théâtre Sarah Bernhardt included Breton, Dullin, Adamov, Barrault and Collette Thomas. He was given lodgings in an old pavilion in the grounds of a private clinic at Ivry-sur-Seine, where he lived for the rest of his life.

After his release, Artaud began to write furiously, day and night. He was to read three of his poems in January 1947 at the Théâtre du Vieux Colombier, but instead he launched into a tirade against his psychiatrists. After seeing a Van Gogh exhibition (he identified with Van Gogh who also spent time in asylums) he wrote one of his most brilliant essays, *Van Gogh, 'suicided' by society*. In November 1947 he began recording *To Have Done with the Judgement of God* for French radio with Paule Thévenin, Roger Blin and Marie Casarès to be broadcast the following February. However, the recording was banned from broadcast the day before it was due to go out, despite furious protests from the artistic community. By this time Artaud was suffering from cancer of the anus and was taking increasing amounts of laudanum for the pain. On the morning of 4 March 1948, he was found dead sitting at the foot of his bed. His funeral, without religious rites, took place at the cemetery at Ivry.

Theory and Practice

The language of theatre

The basic argument of Artaud's correspondence to Rivière was that he lacked the skills to communicate the ideas in his head within conventional poetic structures. He argued that poems which raise important questions but lack formal structures are more deserving of publication than those with perfect form but nothing to say. After this exchange, Artaud began to explore the nature of language and expression with words. Do thoughts consist of words in the mind, or can thoughts exist without words? Can we interpret sensations of the mind and body without language? Can we experience sensations that language is inadequate to express?

In his essay *Production and Metaphysics*, Artaud berates a Western theatre that relies solely on language for communication and pushes everything else into the background. He wrote,

> Dialogue—something written and spoken—does not specifically belong to the stage but to books...
>
> I maintain the stage is a tangible, physical place that needs to be filled and it ought to speak its own concrete language.
>
> I maintain that this physical language, aimed at the senses and independent of speech, must first satisfy the senses. There must be poetry for the senses just as there is for speech, but this physical, tangible language I am referring to is really only theatrical in as far as the thoughts it expresses escape spoken language.

Artaud never abandoned spoken language, but he believed it was given too much prominence in Western theatre. In his *First Manifesto of the Theatre of Cruelty* he said, 'We do not intend to do away with dialogue, but to give words something of the significance they have in dreams.' He did not want to translate words into gestures but to communicate ideas and attitudes with a language of the senses. Words are literary devices that appeal to the rational part of the brain; his physical language of theatre aimed to by-pass the rational mind and appeal directly to the emotions.

Language of the senses

Think of as many ways as you can to communicate to an audience using their sense of:

i. sight

ii. hearing (you can use the voice as well as music and sound effects, but use the sound of the voice rather than the meaning of the words)

iii. touch/feeling (not just through the hands, but you could use textures on the floor or seats, vibrations, temperature, wind and so on)

iv. smell

v. taste

Remember that you are not just communicating words or places but ideas and attitudes to directly invoke emotions in the spectators.

Examples listed by Artaud of 'expressive means useable on stage' are 'music, dance, plastic art, mimicry, mime, gesture, voice inflexion, architecture, lighting and décor'. After he saw Balinese dancers in 1931, he became convinced that traditional performances and rituals of ancient cultures communicated at a primal, emotional level that did not require language or reason. His trip to Mexico was to study tribes that have had little contact with Western society as part of his quest for a poetry of the body. He believed he had found in the Balinese theatre a performance where the director is supreme and 'becomes a kind of organiser, a master of holy ceremonies', where the physical performance is finely detailed and every gesture reproduced with musical precision without interpretation or improvisation by the performer. Everything in the performance works in harmony with everything else, so that 'There is no transition from a gesture to a cry or sound; everything is connected as if through strange channels penetrating right through the mind!'

Creating a physical language
Create a short performance to communicate one of the following:

• fear
• madness

- parental love
- mistrust
- evil

You are not trying to make your audience consciously think or understand your message, but to make them feel something directly. Rather than understanding that you are representing evil, you want them to react instinctively as though they have been confronted with pure evil. Think about how you can combine, for example, amplified sound, movement, vocal sound, music, lighting effects, costumes and props to make them feel something. Think about where you place your actors in relation to your audience (sitting spectators in the dark before a lit stage may not be the best way to get them to react emotionally). If you use dialogue, the sound of the words should communicate more than the words themselves, for instance by using chanting, vocal inflections, repetition, cries of partial or made-up words. Everything must be learned in detail to the smallest gesture so that it can be repeated exactly, like a dance.

Artaud did not find the key to his physical poetry in Mexico. He later worked on the idea that his will—the conscious desire to express himself—was blocking his ability to fully express his thoughts in words, not the words themselves. He was then incarcerated in various asylums, but from his arrival at Rodez to his death, he produced a phenomenal amount of writing. In the forms of poems, essays, letters, drawings and paintings, these works were direct expressions of Artaud's thoughts and feelings expressed poetically. He had discovered his own form that used words, rhythms, pictures, strings of consonants and even the pressure of the pen on the paper to communicate directly what he was feeling.

Theatre of Cruelty

The name 'Theatre of Cruelty' can be thought of as a blanket term for the type of theatre that Artaud wished to create. Artaud always believed in the power of theatre to transform society and despised the idea of theatre as mere entertainment. However he was not interested in promoting any political movement and was totally opposed to the Surrealists' alliance with Communism. Instead he believed that theatre could put people back in touch with natural instincts lost through suppression of the subconscious and over-reliance on reason and intellect. The Surrealists were greatly influenced by Freud, especially his ideas about repressed impulses and the language of dreams, and much of this stayed with Artaud.

Why did Artaud use the name Theatre of Cruelty?

Artaud's clearest description is given in his essay *No More Masterpieces*:

> With this mania we all have today for belittling everything, as soon as I said 'cruelty' everyone took it to mean 'blood'. But a 'theatre of cruelty' means theatre that is difficult and cruel for myself first of all. And on a performing level, it has nothing to do with the cruelty we practise on one another ... but the far more terrible, essential cruelty objects can practise on us. We are not free and the sky can still fall on our heads. And above all else, theatre is made to teach us this.

Artaud saw life as inherently cruel as none of us has any real control over what happens to us—an understandable point of view when you look at his life story—and he believed that theatre should remind us of this. The *First Manifesto of the Theatre of Cruelty* talks of the 'truthful distillation of dreams' and a desire to show man's 'inner world' or 'man viewed metaphysically'. The cruelty also extends to the artist, for whom this painful public display of the deepest hidden elements of his personality is 'difficult and cruel'. He wanted to communicate the torment at the depths of his soul directly to others so that they could feel his pain, not simply understand it. The *First Manifesto* describes some of his proposed methods of achieving this in the theatre, but he never succeeded in putting his ideas properly into practice. His showpiece creations for the Theatre of Cruelty were *The Cenci* on stage, for which he was forced to use a theatre that was far too large and a leading actress cast more for her financial contacts than her performing abilities, and *To Have Done With The Judgement Of God* on radio, which was banned before it was broadcast. His personal failures do not necessarily indicate flaws in his ideas, many of which have been explored successfully by other practitioners since his death.

A Theatre of Cruelty production

Despite his own practical failures, Artaud left detailed notes on how to stage a Theatre of Cruelty production, especially in the *First* and *Second Manifesto of the Theatre of Cruelty*. Although the various elements are dealt with individually here, just as they are in Artaud's own writings, they should all fuse together without any being more important than the others. He wrote that his theatre 'uses moves, harmonies, rhythms, but only up to the point where they can co-operate in a kind of pivotal expression without favouring any particular art' and the effects created should 'overlap from one sense to another, from colour to sound, words to lighting, tremoring gestures to tonality soaring with sound, and so on'.

Content

In *No More Masterpieces*, Artaud wrote,

> We must finally do away with the idea of masterpieces reserved for a so-called elite but incomprehensible to the masses... Past masterpieces are fit for the past, they are no good to us. We have the right to say what has been said and even what has not been said in a way that belongs to us, responding in a direct and straightforward manner to present-day feelings everybody can understand.
>
> It is senseless to criticise the masses for having no sense of the sublime, when we ourselves confuse the sublime with one of those formal, moreover always dead exhibits. And if, for example, the masses today no longer

understand Oedipus Rex, I would venture to say Oedipus Rex is at fault as a play and not the masses.

He wanted a theatre that dealt with subjects from the audiences' everyday lives in a way that everyone could understand. He did not wish to abandon 'what has been said'— such as the stories and the themes of classic plays—but to tell both old and new stories in a way that is relevant to a modern society. His list of potential Theatre of Cruelty productions in the *First Manifesto* included a few classic old plays, including plays by Shakespeare and other Elizabethan playwrights, and Büchner's *Woyzeck*, together with stories from such diverse sources as the Bible and the Marquis de Sade, but the list is preceded with the words 'Disregarding the text, we intend to stage...'. The old messages and stories are retained, but they are said in a new way.

Your Theatre of Cruelty production

Choose either Act I scene 3 or Act IV scene 1 of *Macbeth*. Both of these scenes have magical and ritual elements including chanting, drumming, rhythm, sound effects, music and visual effects written into the text and have potential for incorporating more of Artaud's ideas. Read your chosen scene through several times so you understand fully the story and its meaning. Although you will be 'disregarding the text', you need to know the story so you can reconstruct its message in a different form. During the following exercises, you will work on the different elements of the scene to build it into a Theatre of Cruelty performance. Do not be inhibited by any practical considerations; if you are intending to stage anything from this, whether in class or in front of an audience, you can produce one version to perform and a more elaborate version that you would present if money and facilities were unlimited.

Staging

The *First Manifesto* calls for a complete reconfiguration of the performance space, breaking down all barriers between performers and spectators. Artaud requests a barn or hangar, rather than a conventional theatre space, which should be rebuilt along the lines of places of worship such as churches or Tibetan temples. This is theatre as religion or spirituality; what Peter Brook was later to refer to as 'Holy Theatre'. The spectators are not sat at one end of this room but in the middle (Artaud even puts them on swivel chairs) with the action happening around them. There are no barriers between actor and audience, all are lit by the same light, and effects such as wind, sound effects and flashes of light are directed as much at the audience as at the performers and so are experienced rather than simply observed. Although the performance happens anywhere in the room, special performance areas are reserved at the four cardinal points of the room and a main space in the centre. The performance space does not just use two dimensions—Artaud requested galleries at different heights stretching across the whole room, allowing performers to cross the space at different levels.

Staging your ToC production

You need to find a suitable space in which to stage your scene, which will probably not be a conventional performance space. It could be a barn, empty outbuilding, hangar, boiler room, cellar, disused lavatory ... anywhere that will give you an open, covered space to enclose your performers and audience together. (If this is to be a practical, rather than theoretical, project, do not let artistic enthusiasm blind you to safety considerations, including providing adequate fire exits.) Where would be the best place for your audience to sit to involve them in the performance? Perhaps they could stand instead of sitting, or even move around to follow the action. What is their first impression when they enter the space? Is something happening when they come in? What areas are used by the performers? Do they have their own distinct areas or do they mingle with the audience? Are there catwalks overhead that can be used by performers?

Direction

Artaud wanted to break free of the supremacy of the text and the playwright, and instead to have a combined author-director. This person would be responsible for creating the play and for choreographing every move and sound made by the performers, who would not be permitted to vary their performances at all from what had been rehearsed.

Performers

Some actors may consider that Artaud's idea of a supreme author-director robs the performers of their own creativity. However, whilst they do not create their own interpretation of a role, the performances demanded by Artaud's style of theatre can only be carried out by skilled, talented performers with highly trained and expressive physical and vocal abilities.

Set

The walls of the room should not be decorated and should easily absorb light to show up more clearly what is happening in front of them. Decoration is provided not by scenery but by costumes and various objects around the space; Artaud describes this rather cryptically in the *First Manifesto*: 'Hieroglyphic characters, ritual costume, thirty foot high effigies of King Lear's beard in the storm, musical instruments as tall as men, objects of unknown form and purpose are enough to fulfil this function.'

Lighting

Artaud recognised that the technical equipment available to him was not adequate to carry out some of his ideas. This is in contrast to the current day, where the standard equipment in most theatres can do most of what Artaud wanted, and if intelligent lighting and effects developed for rock concerts are used, it is possible to create effects far beyond even those that Artaud dreamed of. However, his lighting ideas were to create particular effects, not designed simply for spectacle. He wanted to investigate 'the particular action of light on the mind' and for light and colour 'to produce special tonal properties, sensations of heat, cold, anger, fear and so on'. To create these effects, he wanted 'oscillating light effects, new ways of diffusing light in waves, sheet lighting like a flight of fire arrows'. Strobe lighting and moving lights can provide oscillations, and gobos can also be used to project shaped beams of light that, with a small amount of smoke, can look like bars or sheets of light. Laser units can draw pictures in three-dimensional space using light. Light colour in one lantern or even on the whole stage can be changed at the touch of a button. Some intelligent lights can even fade smoothly from one colour to another.

Lighting your ToC production

Lighting is important for making the performance visible and for concentrating attention on the most important areas. Beyond this necessary function, it can also help to communicate meaning and feeling to an audience. Remember that any effects used must contribute towards communicating something specific to the audience. Consider how the following fundamental elements of lighting can be used in your scene:

- **Colour:** different colours will have different associations for your audience, and in many cases these will be instinctive rather than intellectual associations. Even, white light also has a function.
- **Brightness:** try lighting the same scene with very bright light and then with very dim light to see how it produces different effects on the audience. Experiment combining light with shadow.
- **Areas:** consider which areas of the room need to be lit and which are dark at each moment. Think about the effect of hearing sound from a darkened area, and also the effect of light on the spectators themselves.
- **Images:** shadow images from gobos, slides from a projector and moving film images can be used in a performance. These do not have to be projected onto

a screen—moving images on scenery, props and the bodies of performers can be very effective.

- **Heat:** heat is usually an unwelcome bi-product of stage lighting, but it can contribute towards the effect of your performance. If you turn on a bank of parcans facing your spectators, they will feel the heat from them almost instantly.
- **Effects:** look at the effects described by Artaud and think about which of them would be effective in your scene and how they can be created using modern lighting technology.

Sound

Sound technology has also progressed significantly since Artaud's lifetime. He wanted musical instruments that are also props or items of scenery, not that are simply heard playing from offstage or from the orchestra pit. The sounds they make should 'act deeply and directly on our sensibility through the senses' by using 'utterly unusual sound properties and vibrations which present-day musical instruments do not possess, urging us to use ancient or forgotten instruments or to invent new ones'. He mentions producing 'an unbearably piercing sound', but extremely low-frequency sounds can also be very effective for directly producing feelings in the spectator. Modern electronic instruments can produce an almost infinite range of sampled and synthesised sounds that can be triggered by pretty much anything that can close an electrical connection, not just a keyboard. Percussive sounds can be created by hitting various materials together of different sizes and densities. A good brass musician can produce a sound by blowing into different kinds of tubing or piping. Electronic effects units can distort the human voice and any other sound fed into them in myriad ways.

The sound of ToC

Think about how sound can help to put across the meaning of your Theatre of Cruelty production. As with other elements of the production, you are using sound to induce an instinctive reaction from your spectators. Think about how the following can be used in your production:

- **Voice:** the voice is an integral part of the sound of the production and can be used for words, sounds, part-words, screams, noises, chanting and singing.
- **Instruments:** whether these are conventional acoustic instruments, electric and electronic instruments or ones that you have created yourself, explore the range of sounds you can make and find those that produce instinctive reactions from your audience, especially in conjunction with other elements of your production. Examine particularly very high- and low-frequency sounds.
- **Set:** find items that can be used as props or scenery but which also produce sounds that fit with your production when hit, blown, scraped and so on.
- **Amplification:** sounds, including voices, can be amplified through loudspeakers to produce a different effect. These speakers can be placed in different positions, including above, behind and below the audience, as well as in front of them.
- **Effects:** electronic effects from echo and reverb to pitch shift, vocoder and flange can be easily added to any kind of sound from voices and instruments to footsteps and sound effects.

Costume

Modern dress must be avoided, as its associations are in contemporary times. Artaud looked to traditional costumes that he had seen in Balinese theatre and in Mexico and even in our own ancient past, not for a desire to return to the past or to a simpler life but for their natural associations with rituals and spirituality, as well as for their beauty.

Sample Questions

1. Describe how you would use Artaud's Theatre of Cruelty techniques to stage a Shakespeare play that you know well.
2. How can information be transmitted to an audience in a theatre without using words?
3. Do you believe a theatre performance can bypass reason and intellect and appeal directly to the senses? Argue your case with reference to Artaud's ideas.

4 **Bertolt Brecht**

Biography Overview

Eugen Berthold Friedrich Brecht (he later preferred Bertolt or Bert) was born on 10 February 1898 in Augsburg, Bavaria to a middle-class business family. By the time he was twenty-four he had already written a number of plays, including *Baal*, *In the Jungle of Cities* and *Drums in the Night*; the latter was produced at the Munich Kammerspiel in 1922 and won him the Kleist Prize. In the same year, he began directing Arnolt Bronnen's *Vatermord* in Berlin, but withdrew during rehearsals due to arguments over the production (one of the leading actors refused to continue working with him). In 1928, his play *The Threepenny Opera*, written with Elisabeth Hauptmann and with music by Kurt Weill, premiered in Berlin and was a popular success. Erich Engel was the director, but Brecht made significant contributions.

By the 1930s, Brecht was a committed Communist and had started to study Marx. Hitler's Fascists were becoming more powerful, and many left-wing intellectuals in Germany (and in many other countries, including Britain) believed that the only political ideology to present a real alternative to Fascism at that time was Communism. Brecht wrote a series of *Lehrstücke*, or 'teaching plays', for performance to workers, students and children that encouraged Communist thinking beginning with *The Flight over the Ocean* in 1929 and ending with *The Mother* in 1932.

On 27 February 1933, the burning down of the German parliament building, the Reichstag, signalled the beginning of Hitler and the Nazi Party's domination of Germany, and Brecht and his wife Helene Weigel fled Germany the next morning. Two years later the Nazis stripped him of his German citizenship; if he had stayed, they may well have taken his life.

Over the next few years he continued to write and his plays were produced around Europe and in the United States, but he had little or no involvement with any of them as director. In 1939 he was on the move again as the Nazis' gradual occupation of Europe edged closer, and in 1941 he settled in California. He had dreamed about visiting America from being very young, but, although he wrote a number of major plays while he was there, he struggled to work within the American system and most of the proposed films and stage productions he worked on came to nothing. His biggest theatrical success, however, was a collaboration with English actor Charles Laughton on an English translation of *Life of Galileo*. Despite problems understanding one another's language, each admired the other greatly, and the play opened at the Coronet Theatre in Los Angeles on 31 July 1947 with Laughton in the title role. Joseph Losey was named as the director, but his role in the production was secondary to the collaboration between Brecht and Laughton. The play was a major success, but Brecht had by this time attracted the attention of the House Un-American Activities Committee, a government committee set up to root out and silence those in the public eye whose political views were more left-wing than the government would like. Brecht gave a masterful performance to the committee; despite not really answering any of their questions, the chairman thanked him and said he was an example to other witnesses. Despite his success, he left for Paris the next day, then settled in Zurich in November. A year later he set off for East Berlin after being refused a visa for the American zone.

Brecht completed his *Short Organum for the Theatre*, a collection of notes detailing his ideas about theatre, in 1948. In January 1949, Brecht's production of *Mother Courage and her Children* opened at the Deutches Theater, Berlin and Brecht formed the Berliner Ensemble with his wife Helene Weigel as artistic director. After a number of productions at the Deutches Theater, the Berliner Ensemble settled at the Theater am Schiffbauerdamm in March 1954.

Brecht attended his last rehearsal on 10 August 1956. He died on the 14th from a heart infarct on the eve of the Berliner Ensemble's departure for its first, and very successful, appearance in London.

Theory and Practice

Brecht once wrote:

> If the critics could only look at my theatre as the audience does, without starting out by stressing my theories, then they might well simply see theatre—a theatre, I hope, imbued with imagination, humour and meaning—and only when they began to analyse its effects would they be struck by certain innovations, which they could then find explained in my theoretical writings.

Many people still begin learning about Brecht by reading *Brecht on Theatre* and then go away with the view that he was a dull theoretician. However, he was primarily a playwright and a director, and his theoretical writing helped him to work through his ideas about how to improve the effectiveness of his practical work. Some people believe that his later productions were successful *despite* his theoretical work, but this misinterprets both the theory and the theatre of this major theatre practitioner. The main elements of Brecht's epic theatre, although they developed over time, were just as integral to his last production as to his earlier work.

Epic theatre

'Epic theatre' is often used as a blanket term to cover Brecht's theatrical style, but it had previously been used by some of his contemporaries in German theatre such as Piscator and Wedekind. German playwrights Goethe and Schiller published an essay in 1797 called *On Epic and Dramatic Poetry* describing the difference, as they saw it, between dramatic and epic poetry based on Aristotle's *Poetics*. They wrote,

> The actor ... wants the spectators ... to feel the sufferings of his soul and of his body with him, share his embarrassments and forget their own personalities for the sake of his ... The spectator must not be allowed to

rise to thoughtful contemplation; he must passionately follow the action; his imagination is completely silenced.

Goethe and Schiller were describing what Brecht wanted to change in contemporary theatre; he did not want his audiences to empathise with the characters in his plays, as this would prevent them from questioning the characters' actions. He asked in his *Short Organum for the Theatre* (1948), 'How much longer are our souls, leaving our "mere" bodies under cover of the darkness, to plunge into those dreamlike figures up on the stage, there to take part in the crescendos and climaxes which "normal" life denies us?' Brecht called his theatre 'epic' and 'anti-Aristotlean' and defined it in opposition to the 'dramatic' described by Schiller and Goethe. In his notes to accompany his play *The Rise and Fall of the City Mahagonny* that were published in 1930, he included a table contrasting the 'dramatic theatre' with the 'epic theatre'.

Dramatic Theatre	Epic Theatre
plot	narrative
implicates the spectator in a stage situation	turns the spectator into an observer, but
wears down his capacity for action	arouses his capacity for action
provides him with sensations	forces him to take decisions
experience	picture of the world
the spectator is involved in something	he is made to face something
suggestion	argument
instinctive feelings are preserved	brought to the point of recognition
the spectator is in the thick of it, shares the experience	the spectator stands outside, studies
the human being is taken for granted	the human being is the object of the enquiry

he is unalterable	he is alterable and able to alter
eyes on the finish	eyes on the course
one scene makes another	each scene for itself
growth	montage
linear development	in curves
evolutionary determinism	jumps
man as a fixed point	man as a process
thought determines being	social being determines thought
feeling	reason

This was Brecht's earliest attempt to define epic theatre in print. The notes in the table can be boiled down to a few essential points:

- *The spectator is an active, not a passive, part of the performance.* A spectator of a dramatic presentation is encouraged to empathise with the main characters and be carried along by their emotional journey. In epic theatre, the spectator must stand apart from the action and actively take sides and make decisions about the characters and situations.

- *The play does not develop naturally from one action to the next.* In a dramatic piece, each scene springs directly from the one before. In epic theatre, each scene is a separate entity that does not evolve naturally into the next or from the last.

- *The outcome is not inevitable and could have been different.* The natural flow of dramatic theatre implies that the plot is an unstoppable train and once it sets off there is nothing the characters can do to change it. Epic theatre presents us with situations whose outcome depends on conscious decisions made by the characters; if they had made different decisions, the outcome would have been different. The spectators must be made to understand that society is changeable, not fixed.

Epic theatre in practice

Think of an issue, current news story or controversial topic that arouses strong feelings and opposing viewpoints. Create a scene, or a number of scenes, based on this issue, in which the characters are forced to make difficult decisions where each choice would result in a different outcome that forces the spectators to consider the implications of each choice. These should not be easy decisions, nor should you only argue properly the side that you agree with. For instance, Brecht's Mother Courage has to decide whether to sell something to get the money she needs to feed her family or protect her son from being taken by the army recruiter to fight in the war. How can you stage your scene so that:

- your spectators are forced to have an opinion on your characters' actions rather than empathising with them;
- each of your scenes stands alone and does not depend on other scenes;
- the outcome is shown to be the result of decisions made by the characters and is not inevitable?

Towards the end of Brecht's life, he started to believe that epic theatre had become a formal set of tools that could equally be applied to forms of theatre that had nothing to do with his artistic or political ideals. Just before he died, he wrote that epic theatre is an essential starting point for his productions, but 'it does not of itself imply that productivity and mutability of society from which they derive their main element of pleasure'. He was not abandoning the principals or techniques of epic theatre; he simply believed that they were insufficient to fully explain how the theatre he had created achieved its aims. Brecht's theatre had a purpose, which was to show up contradictions and inequalities in society and to show that they could be changed; it was not just an alternative style of presentation. There is some evidence that he was to have adopted the term 'dialectical theatre' instead, but dialectics had been an integral part of Brecht's style for some time.

Dialectics

Brecht often quoted from Karl Marx, 'The philosophers have only *interpreted* the world in various ways; the point is to *change* it.' Marx wanted to explain the structure of society to show that it could be changed. If people believe that society has a natural order and structure that cannot be altered, they will probably accept the way things are; if they believe, like Marx, that the structure of society is man-made and can be changed, some of them may take steps to try to change it. Those in positions of power who are keen to stay there would no doubt prefer the people under them to believe the former rather than the latter.

Brecht was greatly influenced by Marx in his work as well as in his political views and he tried to turn some of Marx's theories into theatrical practice. In his notes on Erwin Strittmater's play *Katzgraben*, Brecht wrote, 'I wanted to take the principle that it was not just a matter of interpreting the world but of changing it, and apply that to theatre.' The opening song to Brecht's play *The Exception and the Rule* ends with:

Please, we say to you now, do not accept

Events that happen every day as natural!

For in these times of bloody confusion

Ordered disorder, deliberate violence

Inhuman humanity—

Nothing must be called natural, so that nothing

May be thought unchangeable.

How can a play show people that they can change society?
In his table comparing dramatic to epic theatre, Brecht rejected 'growth', 'linear development' and 'evolutionary determinism' for 'montage', 'in curves' and 'jumps'. If each action in the play happens as a direct result of previous events, it is implied that it could not have happened any other way. If opposing possibilities are presented forcing the characters (and the spectators) to decide on the best way to proceed, it is clear that the outcome was not inevitable

and would have been different if different choices had been made. Brecht wrote of his characters, 'Whatever he doesn't do must be contained and conserved in what he does. In this way every sentence and every gesture signifies a decision; the character remains under observation and is tested. The technical term for this procedure is "fixing the 'not ... but'".' If the situation shown on stage has direct parallels to the political situation outside the theatre, the spectators learn that they could change events in their society.

Presenting opposites

Look at the scene you created for the previous exercise. Have you presented every side of each decision your characters have to make equally clearly so that your spectators can make their own decisions? Fix the 'not ... but'—your characters should show that they are **not** doing one thing **but** instead doing another.

This presentation of contradictory ideas in order to search for a new idea or course of action is known as dialectics, a subject at the centre of both Marx's and Brecht's theories.

Dialectical Materialism

Dialectical materialism was at the heart of Marx's philosophy, but its history goes back much further than this. The 'Art of Dialectics' was practised in Ancient Greece, where most of Western philosophy, science, mathematics, art and politics began. A dialectical argument begins by putting forward an idea or *thesis* together with a contradictory idea or *antithesis*. The argument is concluded when the contradictions of both original ideas are resolved to form a new idea or *synthesis*.

In the nineteenth century, dialectics was adopted by a number of philosophers including Hegel and Marx. Marx, unlike Hegel, looked at dialectics from a materialist viewpoint; where Hegel believed that ideas could change the material conditions around us, Marx believed that the material world is primary and determines our thoughts and ideas. If you look at the table comparing dramatic to epic theatre again, Brecht rejects a theatre that implies 'thought determines being' for one that shows 'social being determines thought'. In other words, he was trying to create theatre from a materialist viewpoint, showing that people are products of their society.

Dialectical Theatre

In his appendices to the *Short Organum* published after his death, Brecht wrote:

> The bourgeois theatre's performances always aim at smoothing over contradictions, at creating false harmony, at idealisation. Conditions are reported as if they could not be otherwise; characters are individuals, incapable by definition of being divided ... If there is any development it is always steady, never by jerks; the developments always take place within a definite framework which cannot be broken through.
>
> None of this is like reality, so a realistic theatre must give it up.

Brecht attacked naturalistic styles of theatre and claimed that his own style, which constantly reminded spectators of its artifice, was more realistic. He believed that real life is not an unbroken chain of consecutive events and that people do not have fixed characters that always determine their behaviour and the characters in his plays reflect this.

Many actors have great difficulties with this idea and try to create an unbroken through-line, which, of course, weakens the effect that Brecht was trying to create. Just as he did not want his spectators to become absorbed in the play, he also did not want his actors to become absorbed in their roles. He said he wanted his actors to demonstrate their characters to the audience but to also be present as themselves, commenting on the role. Brecht used the following exercise in rehearsal to help his actors to grasp this difficult concept.

> **Actor and role**
> Take a page of dialogue from a play. Perform the script, but after each line the actor must say the words 'he said'

or 'she said' as though it was a page from a novel rather than a play. You could take this exercise further by, for instance, describing to the audience the character's actions and thoughts.

Remember that this is a rehearsal exercise; these additions would not stay in for performances. Exercises like this have helped create a myth that Brecht wanted dry, emotionless performances from his actors. In fact his actors performed with as much passion as those in a naturalistic play, but the emphasis was always on clarity of storytelling rather than emotional display, on making the audience think rather than empathise. To illustrate this, he wrote about a street scene in which an onlooker describes a road accident they have just witnessed.

Street Scene
While you were out today, you witnessed a road accident. Stand in front of a crowd of people and describe exactly what you saw, including what was said by everyone involved. During your description, you may imitate the actions and voices of those in the story—not in an attempt to 'become' the characters but to clarify your story. Think back to when you have described a conversation you have had and, without doing an impression of each person, you changed your voice and body to show who was speaking.

Brecht used contradiction in his writing—by contradicting what would be expected in a naturalistic production, presenting characters with contradictory choices and by showing up contradictions in society. The following is a list of some of the contradictions in the first scene of *Life of Galileo*. You may find more.

- The scene begins with a title, telling the audience what is going to happen before the scene begins.
- A child is fascinated by Galileo's scientific theories but scientists and academics are not interested.

- Galileo's view of how the universe works contradicts the established view.
- Galileo has to choose between furthering his research and paying his bills.
- Galileo's explanations seem to contradict what Andrea sees around him.
- Galileo has to take pupils to pay his bills, but this stops him from doing the work that attracts pupils.
- Ludovico believes science contradicts 'a fellow's good sound commonsense'.
- Galileo needs the money from teaching Ludovico but tries to persuade him not to come.
- Galileo has a choice between staying where he can work without interference for less pay than he needs or going somewhere else where he may be prevented from for speaking about his theories.
- Andrea has a choice between coming back without the lenses and losing his winter coat.
- Galileo states that all of the beliefs that his society is built on are open to be questioned and many may be found to be false.
- He warns Andrea not to tell people about what they believe to be true.

Finding contradictions

Read the first scene of *Mother Courage and her Children* and write down all the contradictions you can find. How could you make these contradictions more obvious in performance?

Alienation

The word 'alienation' as a translation of Brecht's word *Verfremdung* has often caused confusion. Because of this, alternative words are sometimes used which are often inadequate to describe Brecht's concept and cause just as much confusion. He was not, as some have mistakenly assumed in the past, seeking to alienate his audiences, but to make familiar occurrences seem strange or unusual.

Brecht wrote in the *Short Organum*, 'A representation that alienates is one which allows us to recognise its subject, but at the same time makes it seem unfamiliar.' As an example, he tells a story about Galileo observing a swinging chandelier:

> He was amazed by this pendulum motion, as if he had not expected it and could not understand its occurring, and this enabled him to come on the rules by which it was governed.

Galileo was looking at an occurrence so common that everyone else accepted it as natural and never thought to question why it happened. Galileo did question it, and he made some of the most significant scientific discoveries in history. Brecht observed, 'it seems impossible to alter what has long not been altered', but if the accepted and the everyday are made to seem unfamiliar and strange, the reasons for things being the way they are can be questioned and the situation can be seen to be alterable. We therefore go back to one of the central points of epic theatre: to make events appear changeable, not inevitable.

How can a play make an audience look at something familiar as though it was something unusual?

Brecht's *Verfremdungseffekt*, or alienation effect, attempted to resolve the contradictory (or dialectical) aims of showing a realistic scene in sufficient detail for the audience to recognise it while emphasising to them that this is a play in a theatre and not a slice of real life. Some of the methods Brecht used were:

- **Plot:** the plays are episodic, with each scene constituting a complete entity that does not evolve from the last scene or into the next. A subtitle was often projected onto a curtain at the beginning of a scene to tell the audience what was going to happen. They were therefore watching to see not what happened, but how it happened and why. Many of Brecht's plays had a historical setting but reflected an issue in the modern world, putting a historical distance between the play and the events Brecht was commenting on.

- **Design:** the design is in 'artistic abbreviation'—in other words there are only sufficient props, costumes and scenery to indicate where and who the characters are. The actors use every element of the design; nothing is there merely for decoration. If a prop has social significance, such as a craftsman's tool of trade (for example the cook's knife in *Mother Courage*), it must be a real, usable object and the actor must learn to use it like an expert. Historical accuracy is not important.

- **Technical:** the set did not try to hide any technical equipment such as lights and cables, which emphasised to the audience that they were in a theatre. One of Brecht's trademarks was a white half-curtain. As it only went up halfway, the curtain track was visible and some larger pieces of scenery could be seen over it being moved. For lighting, Brecht favoured an even white covering that did not create a mood or atmosphere.

- **Songs:** although in real life people do not sing instead of talking at moments of high emotion, in musical theatre, dialogue and music are usually integrated seamlessly together so that the spectator is carried along from dialogue into song without being jolted out of the world of the play. In Brecht's plays, the songs interrupt the action and stand apart from the scene they are in.

- **Acting:** to prevent the audience from becoming absorbed in the characters, the actors should not disappear into their roles, so 'that the actor appears on the stage in a double role, as Laughton and as Galileo; that the showman Laughton does not disappear in the Galileo whom he is showing'. Brecht uses the word 'showing' rather than 'acting' or 'playing' to emphasise that the actor stands on stage as himself demonstrating the character to the audience. Just like with scenery, movement and gesture are kept to a minimum so that when the actors do move it is more significant.

Using alienation techniques

A woman comes home to find her son and his friends printing leaflets for an illegal organisation. This organisation is against everything she has been brought up to believe is right, and she argues with him about his activities. There is a knock at the door; it is the police. If her son is even found with a printing press, let alone the leaflets, he will be taken away by the police, tortured and possibly executed. She has to choose between helping the organisation to conceal its activities and giving her son away to the police.

Stage the above story in two different ways: as a straightforward naturalistic scene, and using as many of Brecht's alienation techniques as possible. How is the audience's role in each performance different?

Gest

Gestus and *gestiche*—usually translated into English as 'gest' and 'gestic'—are terms used by Brecht for something that indicates the attitude of a character. This could be gesture, actions, words, tone of voice or even music.

Interruptions

Walter Benjamin, renowned German critic and friend of Brecht, claimed that epic theatre depends on interruption, and that interruption is one of its most important innovations. By this he meant stopping the action on stage to allow the attitudes of the characters to be analysed. The following is similar to an example he gave.

Create a scene involving three or four characters in which an argument between some of them develops from a minor disagreement into a blazing row, whilst others try to calm the situation. Just as the scene is about to descend into violence, someone else enters and everyone freezes in their tracks at the sight of the newcomer.

This could be a naturalistic scene, but the frozen moment stops the action to allow the audience to take in each character's attitude. Keep your actors frozen and examine their attitudes now. Could changing their positions heighten these attitudes?

In *On Gestic Music*, probably written in the mid-1930s, Brecht wrote:

'Gest' is not supposed to mean gesticulation: it is not a matter of explanatory or emphatic movements of the hands, but of overall attitudes. A language is gestic when it is grounded in a gest and conveys particular attitudes adopted by the speaker towards other men.

Here he indicates the particular attitudes he was most interested in: those adopted by one character towards another, which he called 'social gests'. He wrote in the *Short Organum*,

The realm of attitudes adopted by the characters towards one another is what we call the realm of gest. Physical attitude, tone of voice and facial expression are all determined by a social gest: the characters are cursing, flattering, instructing one another, and so on.

Brecht said that not all gests are social gests; the gest of trying to keep your balance on a slippery surface is not, in itself, a social gest, but it could become one if falling over meant humiliation in front of others (he used the term 'losing one's market value', which shows that he was viewing the technique from a Marxist perspective). The pomp of the Fascists was, he said, a 'hollow gest' as it was just an empty display, but 'Only when the strutting takes place over corpses do we get the social gest of Fascism,' as the presence of the corpses shows the Fascists' attitude towards others (remember that Brecht was writing this whilst in exile from Nazi Germany).

Forming gests
In a small group, choose three words at random from the following list. For each, choose someone to be the

director; this person has to mould the rest of the group into a frozen image to represent that word. Manipulate carefully each person's position, gesture, facial expression and relationship to other people and objects to show clearly their attitude in the image.

The words are: pain; work; poverty; leisure; suspicion; domination; home; power; ignorance.

Look at the images you have created. Which of them do you think show a social gest? Could the others be changed to become social gests?

What use are gests in staging a performance?

To Brecht, these gestic moments are the thread on which the story hangs. He said in the *Short Organum*, 'Splitting such material into one gest after another, the actor masters his character by first mastering the "story".' And that, 'The "story" is the theatre's great operation, the complete fitting together of all the gestic incidents.' He said the actor should search for and be amazed by the inconsistencies in the character's various attitudes, which looks at character dialectically.

Finding gests in a scene

Read the second scene of *The Mother* up to the song. Create a series of frozen images, like in the previous exercise, that represent the main points in the story and show the attitudes of the characters. Choose a word or line from the script to go with each image (if anything is being spoken at that moment). Run the images one after the other by showing the frozen image then unfreezing and saying the line that accompanies it. Does each image demonstrate a social gest? Does the sequence tell the story of the scene? Add or change images if not.

Lehrstücke

The *Lehrstück* (plural: *Lehrstücke*) or 'teaching play' was a type of play written by Brecht between 1929 and 1932 with the purpose of instructing the audience and the performers.

However Brecht said towards the end of his life that these plays were not to put forward a personal point of view but rather were exercises of the mind, to train people to think dialectically.

The *Lehrstücke* came from a particular political point of view; that the state oppressed the workers and the workers needed to learn how to live in the Communist state that would inevitably arise from the current political struggle. It is easy to look back from the next century and view this assumption as naïve and the messages in the plays as strange, as they refer to things that have no relevance in our world today. These plays and their messages were very relevant in pre-war Germany, however, which was one reason why Brecht had to leave the country when the Nazis took power. The very nature of the *Lehrstücke* means that they rarely retain their relevance when seen from outside the time or social context for which they were written. Brecht understood this when he said, 'It is full of mistakes with respect to our time and its virtues, and it is unusable for other times.' Despite this, the *Lehrstück* form can still be a powerful tool if filled with content with contemporary resonances.

These plays should not be thought of as immature works of the young Brecht or as stepping-stones towards his later works in a more familiar theatrical style (the *Schaustück*); they are fully formed examples of epic theatre. He wrote, 'The *Lehrstück* rests on the expectation that the actors may be socially influenced by executing certain attitudes and repeating certain speech patterns.' Therefore the plays were written to teach the groups of people who performed them, not those who watched them. Brecht looked on these early works as the future of theatre even later in his life, and they were extremely influential on many later theatre practitioners such as Heiner Müller and Augusto Boal, as well as on the theatre-in-education movement. In many ways, Brecht believed his later works to be a great step backwards, but the world changed a great deal during his lifetime and he knew that the form of his plays, as well as their content, would have to change in order to communicate his messages to the audiences he wanted to reach.

The Flight Over the Ocean (originally titled *Lindbergh's Flight* until the aviator Lindberg's sympathies with the Nazis became known)—'A radio "Lehrstück" for boys and girls'—was performed at the Baden—Baden Music Festival in 1929. All of the parts apart from the airman were to be broadcast on the radio, and the airman's part was to be sung and spoken by the listener. To have a group play a single character also is an alienation device that prevents empathy with, or hero worship of, a single central character. The theme of self-sacrifice for the greater good was an important part of Communist thinking, and Brecht brought this out even more in the *Lehrstücke He Said Yes* and *The Decision* (also translated as *The Measures Taken*). In both plays, the individual has to give his life willingly for the project to continue. In the questionnaires that Brecht asked audience members to complete after a performance, a school class disagreed strongly with the ending of *He Said Yes*, so Brecht wrote *He Said No* in which the character refuses to give his life. Rather than reversing the message of the earlier play, the story was modified to promote the idea that old traditions need to be reworked to fit the modern world, and both plays were usually performed together.

Model books

Brecht once wrote about his plays,

> As it is not so much a new school of playwriting as a new way of performance being tried out on an old play, our new adaptation cannot be handed over in the usual way to theatres to do what they like with. An obligatory model production has been worked out, which can be grasped from a collection of photographs accompanied by explanatory instructions.

This was in the introduction to the first of his 'model books', in this case for *Antigone*. He believed that his most important innovations were in the production, not the writing, of his plays and so it was not sufficient to publish his scripts alone and expect future directors to be able to stage them effectively. He therefore produced model books for many of his later productions, consisting of a script supplemented by a large number of photographs and extensive notes on his own staging of the play. In 1949, he said, 'As it stands *Mother Courage* can be staged in the old way ... But this would certainly mean doing without the quite specific effects of such a play, and its social function would misfire.' These effects and methods of achieving them were detailed in the *Couragemodell*.

Why would a director want to use someone else's production rather than creating their own?

Brecht did not want his model books to be used to create 'museum' productions that recreate his own productions down to the finest details as they were conceived for his actors and audience. On the other hand, some directors have reacted against being told how to stage the play by the writer by making their production as different from the one described by Brecht as they could. Both of these approaches misunderstand Brecht's intentions when creating the model books and result in productions that fail to communicate the ideas at the heart of the plays. Brecht anticipated these problems; he warned in the *Couragemodell* about,

> those who take [the model books] up without having learnt how to use them. Meant to simplify matters, they are not simple to handle. They are intended not to render thought unnecessary but to provoke it: not as a substitute to artistic creation but as its stimulus.

He wanted other directors to see what he was trying to achieve with his production and then build on his methods or substitute them for better ones. He likened this to advances in science and technology, where each advance is built on the foundations of earlier discoveries so that each scientist does not have to rediscover basic principles before creating anything new. Brecht himself worked using this principle, even on his own plays. He used Teo Otto's designs from the Zurich Schauspielhaus production of *Mother Courage* in 1939 as the basis for his own production ten years later, right down to the arrangement of props, scenery and people. In the 1950 Munich production of the same play, Therese Giehse took the character of Courage as played by Brecht's wife Helene Weigel and described in *Couragemodell* and made, according to Brecht, 'beautiful additions' to it. Brecht saw this as evidence that the model books could work as he wanted them to. Weigel later adopted some of Giehse's additions in Brecht's own production.

Excerpts from six of these model books together with some additional notes form the book *Theaterarbeit*, which unfortunately has still not been translated into English as a whole volume. *Theaterarbeit* summarises some uses of the model book for a production:

1. The modelbook shows the basic gest of a play.
2. The modelbook demonstrates the scenic arrangements related by the play's plot.
3. The modelbook shows the treatment of details.
4. The modelbook warns against mistakes in execution.
5. The modelbook facilitates the division of the plot, e.g., the precise parsing of the plot elements.
6. The modelbook gives tempo and running times for the production.

Couragemodell

In *Theaterarbeit*, Brecht declared the first stage of creating a production to be 'Analysis of the Play', part of which involves:

> Boil the story down to half a sheet of paper. Then divide it into separate episodes, establishing the nodal points, i.e. the important events that carry the story a stage further. Then examine the relationship of the episodes, their construction.

It can be seen from the model books that this is precisely what Brecht did. An important part of this analysis to Brecht was to find ways of bringing out the social significance of the play and the separate episodes.

Breaking down the story

Think of a story that you know well from a play, book or film. Now apply Brecht's method of analysis to it:

- Summarise the story in half a page, making sure you cover all of the most important story elements.
- Divide your summary into separate episodes or story units. These may coincide with scenes or chapters, but a scene may contain two distinct units of a story, or an episode may continue over one or more scenes, especially in a film.
- Identify the key points or events that significantly change or advance the story.
- Examine the relationship between these key points to see how the story works. Think about how you would stage these key points to make them effective and emphasise their importance to an audience.

Now read Brecht's play *Mother Courage and her Children* and break it down in the same way.

Brecht began his analysis by giving each scene a title. This should not be confused with the title shown to the audience at the opening of each scene in many of Brecht's plays, designed to focus the audience on the important elements of the plot, and to link them with the characters and their social and political situation. The titles used for analysis are short, describing the action in as few words as possible, and when they are put together, they summarise the action of the whole play.

Staging key points

Create a still image for each of the key points that you identified in the last exercise for your chosen story using the people in your group. Reposition people and objects until you are satisfied that they are arranged in the most effective way to communicate the story at that point to an audience. Do not forget gestures, facial expressions

> or the social relationship between characters. Repeat this
> for *Mother Courage.*

In the *Couragemodell*, Brecht broke the story into twelve episodes corresponding to the twelve scenes:

1. The business woman Anna Fierling, known as Mother Courage, encounters the Swedish army.
2. Before the fortress of Wallhof Mother Courage meets her brave son again.
3. Mother Courage switches from the Lutheran to the Catholic camp and loses her honest son Swiss Cheese.
4. The Song of the Grand Capitulation.
5. Mother Courage loses four officers' shirts and dumb Kattrin finds a baby.
6. Prosperity has set in, but Kattrin is disfigured.
7. Mother Courage at the peak of her business career.
8. Peace threatens to ruin Mother Courage's business. Her dashing son performs one heroic deed too many and comes to a sticky end.
9. Times are hard, the war is going badly. On account of her daughter, she refuses the offer of a home.
10. Still on the road.
11. Dumb Kattrin saves the city of Halle.
12. Mother Courage moves on.

Just as these scene titles, when put together, summarise the story of the play, Brecht took each of these scenes and summarised them further to describe the action within each scene, again as briefly as possible but including every important action. For instance, scene eleven is summarised as:

A surprise attack is planned on the city of Halle; soldiers force a young peasant to show them the way. The peasant and his wife tell Kattrin to join them in praying for the city. Kattrin climbs up on the barn roof and beats the drum to awaken the city. Neither the offer to spare her mother in the city nor the threat to smash the cart can make her stop drumming. Death of dumb Kattrin.

Brecht's scene breakdown

Reread scene eleven of *Mother Courage*. Take each of the five sentences in the above summary and create a frozen image from it. Again rearrange the composition of people and objects to make each image as effective as you can make it. Run the images one after the other to show the story of the scene in still pictures.

Brecht expanded each of these sentences still further to add more detail. 'Kattrin climbs up on the barn roof and beats the drum to awaken the city' becomes,

> From the peasant woman's prayer Kattrin learns that the children in Halle are in danger. Stealthily she takes the drum from the cart, the same drum she had brought back when she was disfigured. With it she climbs up on the barn roof. She starts drumming. The peasants try in vain to make her stop.

The model contains many additional notes on the staging of each scene. Most scenes contain at least one section headed 'A detail', and Brecht often uses the words 'fully acted out' when he wants an action to be spelled out clearly rather than rushed. Under the heading 'On details' he wrote, 'On the brightly lighted stage every detail, even the smallest, must of course be acted out to the full. This is especially true of actions which on our stage are glossed over.' For instance, the stage direction at the end of scene nine reads,

> They both [Courage and Kattrin] harness themselves to the cart, then wheel it round and drag it off. When the cook arrives he looks blankly at his kit.

This is a simple series of actions that could be over in seconds. Under the heading 'The cook sets out for Utrecht' in the model, Brecht insisted that,

> Scenes of this kind must be fully acted out: Courage and Kattrin harness themselves to the cart, push it back a few feet so as to be able to circle the parsonage, and then move off to the right. The cook comes out, still chewing

a piece of bread, sees his belongings, picks them up and goes off to the rear with long steps. We see him disappear. The parting of the ways is made visible.

Brecht has expanded on his simple stage direction by setting out a sequence of actions that give the scene depth and clarity. He explains very simply what he is trying to achieve—to make visible the parting of the cook and Mother Courage. The actions described in the stage direction may seem simple, but they indicate a life-changing moment in which two people who almost lived together separate, forever, and this significance should be apparent from the staging.

Breaking down another scene
Reread scene one of *Mother Courage*.

- Summarise the main action of the scene in as few words as possible.
- Take each sentence of your summary and create a frozen image from it. Run these images one after the other to make sure they are as effective as possible and they tell the full story of the scene.
- Make notes on the details of the staging of each moment as you break down each sentence. Stage the scene with actors moving and speaking the lines, and add to or change your notes as you work on the scene.

Take your time with this exercise and keep changing your staging and your notes until you have the most effective staging of the scene you can create.

If you look at the notes from the *Couragemodell* you may notice that dialogue is rarely mentioned. The model books describe a very visual, pictorial method of staging, where the arrangement of actors and objects can have more significance than the words spoken. Brecht wrote that a scene should be perfectly understandable by an audience watching it from the other side of a glass wall—in other words, still understandable even if the audience is unable to hear a single word spoken by the actors. If a scene was not working in rehearsal, the first thing he did was rearrange the blocking. This visual approach was also evident by his relationship with his designers, particularly his school friend Caspar Neher. Neher would not just plan the layout of scenery and props when designing a scene but would also design the arrangement of actors within it. There is an account of a rehearsal in which Brecht abandoned work on a particular scene until Neher could get there because he could not get the blocking correct without him.

Sample Questions

1. What are the advantages and disadvantages of using a model book when creating a new production of a play?
2. Compare and contrast Brecht's method of breaking down a play for performance with that of Stanislavski.

5 Jerzy Grotowski

Biography Overview

Jerzy Grotowski was born on 11 August 1933 in Rzeszów in eastern Poland. His father was a painter and sculptor from Kraków who worked in forestry and his mother was a schoolteacher. They lived in Przemysl until September 1939 when Germany invaded Poland, triggering the start of World War II. When the war began, his father was an officer in the Polish Army. Grotowski moved with his mother, Emilia Grotowska, and his older brother, Kasimierz, to Nienadówka near Rzeszów where they remained until the end of the war. Grotowski attended a school in Nienadówka, where his mother taught.

At the age of sixteen, Grotowski became very ill and spent a year in hospital. Before this he was very active, in particular, a keen swimmer, but he read many books and became much more studious during his illness and decided to devote himself to art. He gave poetry recitals in nearby towns, winning a number of prizes for his poems, and became a Communist and a member of the Association of Polish Youth. In 1951 he graduated from high school and decided he wanted to become a theatre director. By this time his family had moved to Kraków, and he had got a job as a clerk in a district court working on insurance claims. He applied to the acting programme at the State Theatre School in Kraków to gain experience as an actor before training as a director. He was accepted on the basis of his written essay for the entrance examination and his high school report, but was denied any financial aid.

While on the acting course from October 1951 to June 1955, Grotowski also went to lectures for his growing interest in Eastern culture and philosophy, and for a time he considered leaving the theatre course for one on either East Asia or medicine. In his fourth year, he played Pyotr in

The Smug Citizen by Gorky and directed a collage of excerpts from various plays by Juliusz Slowacki entitled *Love Scenes*. He completed his acting degree in 1955 and went on to study directing for a year at the State Institute of Theatre Arts (GITIS) in Moscow, where he directed a number of plays and studied the work of Stanislavski, Meierhold, Vakhtangov and Tairov. His professional directorial debut was in April 1957, co-directing Eugene Ionesco's *The Chairs* at Kraków with Aleksandra Mianowska, and he directed a number of stage and radio plays over the next couple of years including Anton Chekhov's *Uncle Vanya*.

In 1959, Grotowski was invited by critic and theorist Ludwik Flaszen to be the stage director at Theatre of 13 Rows in Opole. In 1961, Grotowski staged the Polish classic *Forefather's Eve* by Adam Mickiewicz, and he broke up the thirteen rows of the auditorium into small groupings of moveable chairs through which the actors moved and performed. The company became Laboratory Theatre of 13 Rows in March 1962, and went on to create famous productions of *Akropolis* by Stanislaw Wyspianski in 1962, *Dr Faustus* by Christopher Marlowe in 1963, *The Constant Prince* by Pedro Calderon de la Barca in 1965 and *Apocalypsis cum figuris* in 1969. Productions were often taken off for further work and re-launched; other productions were worked on for months or years and never put before the public. When Grotowski's company was performing *Faustus* in Lodz, Eugenio Barba paid for an illegal trip to see it for the delegates of the Warsaw 1963 International Theatre Institute meeting, which suddenly brought notoriety and respect for Grotowski's work from the world outside Poland.

In January 1965, the Laboratory Theatre moved to an intimate theatre space in Wroclaw in southern Poland. Grotowski was already finding it difficult to create theatre productions, and after he returned from his 1969 tour of America he declared that he had 'crossed a barrier' into a 'post-theatrical epoch'; this was when he moved from a Theatre of Productions (a theatre for performance before an audience) to Paratheatre. *Apocalypsis* was cited by Grotowski as a key project that moved his work to a different level, but he had also spent some time travelling through India and Kurdistan, seeing places and meeting people. He began to believe that a search for truth could not be served by pretending to experience something on a stage in order to earn applause. Paratheatre does not have stories or characters or even an audience; it is an attempt to remove all barriers between people in a group in order to achieve communication at the deepest level. The work often took place in forests or on hilltops and would include anyone who wished to feel 'open'; numbers of participants grew, reaching their height in 1974 with the 'University of Research' of the Theatre of Nations in Wroclaw, which involved over 4,500 people. In the second half of the 1970s while members of the Laboratory were still involved in Paratheatre, Grotowski began the next phase of his work: the Theatre of Sources. In this, he worked with a group of thirty-six people from 1977 to 1980 from widely differing backgrounds including the United States, India, Poland, Bangladesh, Japan, France and Haiti to find ways of communicating that transcend language and culture.

Martial law was declared in Poland in 1981, and Grotowski left the country the following year after arranging for his colleagues from the Laboratory Theatre to be working outside the country so that the government could not prevent them from leaving in reaction to his defection. He arrived in the United States via Italy and Haiti and claimed asylum. From 1982–3, he held a position at Columbia University and began to develop his ideas for Objective Drama for New York University assisted by Richard Schechner, but the money for the programme did not appear and so he accepted an invitation from the University of California-Irvine to continue his work there. Grotowski turned to the form he called Objective Drama because he believed that art had lost its ancient purpose to stabilise and make coherent a society and to pass traditions and cultural knowledge from one generation to the next. While modern performance is effective in communicating personal emotion and psychology, 'it is failing, by and large, to develop its function as a cohesive force expressing the shared human need for values, identity and community. More and more these are made into a purely individual search ... and society, as a result, fragments.' Grotowski described what he was searching for in an interview in the Los Angeles Times:

> To re-evoke a very ancient form of art where ritual and artistic creation were seamless. Where poetry was song, song was incantation, movement was dance. Pre-differentiation Art, if you will, which was extremely powerful in its impact. By touching that, without concern for philosophical or theological motivation, each of us could find his own connection.

He employed non-Western practitioners, explored ancient forms of song, dance and examined ritual and childhood memories to find forms whose effects on the practitioner are objective (determinable and predictable) rather than subjective (unpredictable and different for each individual). For Objective Drama to be of value, Grotowski believed that the participants had to be highly skilled in their respective fields, the research must be conducted in a closed environment and there would be no public performance at the end. He only began to achieve his aims during the third and final year of his residence at California in 1985–6, but then in 1986 he moved to Italy. The Irvine programme continued until 1992, although Grotowski's active participation was infrequent, but the emphasis shifted towards techniques in acting, the director's work with actors and ways of creating meaning in the spectators' perception.

In Pontedera, Italy he set up the Workcenter of Jerzy Grotowski to develop a new project, *Art as vehicle*, named after Peter Brook's 1987 talk 'Grotowski, Art as a vehicle' in which he said,

> It seems to me that Grotowski is showing us something which existed in the past but has been forgotten over the centuries. That is that one of the vehicles which allows man to have access to another level of perception is to be found in the art of performance.

The Workcenter accepted artists from the hundreds of applicants from around the world who committed themselves to a minimum of one year's intensive research, working six days per week and a minimum of eight hours per day. They were split into two groups known as Upstairs and Downstairs, which simply referred to the floor of the building on which they were based. The Downstairs Group was originally led by the American Thomas Richards, who used African and Afro-Caribbean traditions, and the Upstairs Group by Haitian Maud Robart, who looked at traditional Haitian styles of performance and their roots. Funding cuts in 1993 meant that there was only sufficient money for Richards's group to continue. Grotowski described the focus of Art as vehicle as, 'actions related to very ancient songs which traditionally served ritual purposes and so can have a direct impact on—so to say—the head, the heart and the body of the doers'. Where Art as Performance tries to form a particular perception in the minds of the spectators, Art as vehicle works on the performer instead. For this work, Grotowski believed that a rigid structure was necessary together with great attention to precision and performance craft, just as with the best Art as Performance for an audience.

By the late 1990s, Grotowski's health was rapidly deteriorating due to a degenerative heart condition and he died on 15 January 1999. However he had already begun to hand over much responsibility to Richards in his last years and Richards continues to run the Art as vehicle programme at the Workcenter.

Theory and Practice

Poor Theatre

Grotowski's book, *Towards a Poor Theatre*, was published in 1968 towards the end of his Theatre of Productions phase. His theatre was poor in a very real sense; it was funded by the state, but there were times when the company did not have enough money to pay its actors. However the poverty Grotowski referred to in his title described the aesthetic principles that his company had developed and not its financial situation. He described a 'Rich Theatre' that 'depends on artistic kleptomania'—in other words it borrows techniques ('montage, instantaneous change of place, etc') and technology ('movie screens onstage, for example') from other art forms, particularly television and film. He wrote, 'No matter how much theatre expands and exploits its mechanical resources, it will remain technologically inferior to film and television. Consequently, I propose poverty in theatre.' He describes attempts to create a 'total theatre' that combines techniques from different media as 'nonsense'. Poor Theatre, by contrast, boils down the theatrical performance to only those elements that are essential and unique to live theatre: 'we are trying to avoid eclecticism, trying to resist thinking of theatre as a composite of disciplines. We are seeking to define what is distinctly theatre, what separates this activity from other categories of performance and spectacle.'

Finding the essentials

- List all of the different *elements* that can form part of a live theatrical performance, such as actors, make-up, stage, script and so on.
- For each *element*, list its *uses*, for instance, make-up is used to reduce the glare of stage lighting and to help create a character visually.
- Consider whether you feel each use is an essential component of a theatre performance, and also try to think of other, non-technical methods of creating a similar effect, for instance instead of character make-up, Grotowski's actors created character masks just using the muscles of the face.

Grotowski stated:

By gradually eliminating whatever proved superfluous, we found that theatre can exist without make-up, without autonomic costume and scenography, without a separate performance area (stage), without lighting and sound effects, etc. It cannot exist without the actor-spectator relationship of perceptual, direct, "live" communion.

All elements of performance apart from actor and spectator are supplementary—even the text of the play. He wrote, 'But can the theatre exist without actors? I know of no example. ... Can the theatre exist without an audience? At least one spectator is needed to make it a performance ... We can thus define theatre as "what takes place between spectator and actor".' Theatre cannot exist without the actor and the spectator, and the close, live contact between the two is what distinguishes theatre from television and film. Grotowski's later work without audiences may seem to contradict this, but the principle of finding what is essential and getting rid of everything else, a process he called *via negativa*, is at the heart of everything that Grotowski ever did. He described his art as being more like sculpture than painting, because painting builds its image by adding colours to a blank canvas, whereas sculpture removes excess material to reveal something that already existed within the original block of stone.

Training the Actor

Grotowski's *via negativa* approach to theatre focuses strongly on the actor's performance, as most other elements of theatrical production are eliminated or reduced to their essentials (he wrote, 'we consider the personal and scenic technique of the actor as the core of theatre art'). However *via negativa* is also applied to the training of the actor: the actor searches for physical or psychological impediments to achieving his or her goals and tries to eradicate them rather than learning new techniques and skills. In the introduction to the section on actor training in *Towards a Poor Theatre* he wrote:

> All the exercises which merely constituted an answer to the question: 'How can this be done?' were eliminated ... The actor must discover those resistances and obstacles which hinder him in his creative task ... The actor no longer asks himself: 'How can I do this?'. Instead, he must know what **not** to do, what obstructs him.

Grotowski's actors had a very long and physically demanding training schedule and were expected to constantly extend the boundaries of their physical capabilities. To Grotowski, great art did not consist of close reproductions of everyday behaviour and speech, and his actors were expected to perform 'magical acts (which the audience is incapable of reproducing)'. He believed that an actor's training is always ongoing, and actors in his company would train every day, not to prepare for playing a particular role but as part of a constant process of their work on themselves (as Stanislavski referred to it).

Grotowski includes a number of exercises for actors to use in their training in *Poor Theatre*—in fact they fill a large section of the book. However he later became very wary of publishing specific details of exercises, as he was concerned that they were being used as a formula, rather than as a preparation, for true creativity. Grotowski believed that no system of exercises could make an actor creative; exercises are valuable for preparing the actor's body for physical and vocal expression and for addressing and improving on specific limitations in an actor's abilities, but they are not, in themselves, a magical path to creativity.

The exercises in *Towards a Poor Theatre* are divided into four areas:

- Physical exercises (warm-ups, exercises on specific parts of the body, exercises to improve physical agility and stamina).
- Plastic exercises (performing various physical tasks in different ways such as walking, jumping, gestures etc).
- Exercises of the facial mask (exercises to improve control and expressivity of the facial muscles).
- Technique of the voice (breathing, projection and voice production).

The exercises that Grotowski developed with his collaborators became known as *corporels*. The content of these exercises is not unique to Grotowski—in fact he credits many of his influences including Hatha Yoga, Dalcroze's Eurhythmics, Delsarte, Kathakali (classical Indian theatre), Charles Dullin, Meyerhold's biomechanics and Stanislavski's Method of Physical Actions. The difference between Grotowski's actor training and other training using similar exercises is in the approach to and the motivation behind their execution. Grotowski fiercely rejected any form of training that gave an actor a range of different skills to display, such as mime, stage fighting, diction, dance and so on. This sort of training does not teach the actor to be creative but will simply enable him or her to skilfully carry out instructions in that discipline from someone else. Actors trained in this way may perform with great virtuosity and technical ability but without any living *impulse*—Grotowski's term for something that starts inside the actor's body and then extends outwards to become a physical action. For Grotowski's actors, impulses *always* precede physical actions. They are continually stretching their physical abilities and extending their limits, whilst at the same time developing their imaginative capabilities and their instinctive responses to both tangible and remembered stimuli. For this reason, Grotowski described these training techniques as *psychophysical*. Although many of the exercises are physically demanding, the aim is not to learn to execute them with technical perfection but to remove all barriers that prevent the body from expressing fully every impulse that may arise within the actor. Grotowski wrote:

> The actor ... must be able to manifest the least impulse. He must be able to express, through sound and movement, those impulses which waver on the borderline between dream and reality.

Corporal exercises

Choose some physical exercises involving balance, such as headstands and shoulder stands, to work on—something that you find difficult, but not impossible with practice. Work on them for as long as it takes to master the physical techniques that enable you to perform the exercise correctly. This is the first stage, in which you push the limits of your physical ability and learn the exercises in a disciplined and technical manner. Once you have found the correct position for each exercise, experiment with moving your spine to displace your balance to find where the limits in your body's equilibrium lie. Now you are using a general exercise to explore the capabilities and limitations of your own body. While you are performing the exercise, create, in your mind, some *associations* for the actions you are carrying out – in other words, find a motivation or justification for what you are doing beyond the physical training requirement to stop it being simply a mechanical, repetitive movement. For instance, if you are performing sit-ups, think about what you could be reaching for. As with Stanislavski's exercises, associations should be specific and not general; something important that gives you the impulse to carry out the exercise. You can change it at any time. With a partner, construct an improvised 'dialogue' using elements of the exercises you have been practising. This sequence must be improvised, not planned or rehearsed, and you should try to find a flow in your movements together without losing the precision of the positions you have been practising.

Another set of exercises used by Grotowski was the *plastiques*, which were less physically demanding than the corporal exercises but which focussed more on precision of detailed movements. The movements used were based on systems of actor training by European practitioners such as Dalcroze and Delsarte. They began as impulses in the spine that worked outwards to move another part of the body such as the wrist, the shoulders or the chest, and the actor had to learn them and repeat them with precision. As with the corporal exercises, the actors put these movements together in different ways in an improvised dialogue in response to each other or to externally introduced stimuli. Here we can see two of Grotowski's important principles: the apparently contradictory combination of rigidly defined movement and improvisation, and the importance of maintaining contact with something outside the actor's body whether present in the room, such as another person, or conjured from the actor's memory or imagination. On one level, the exercises train the actor's body to extend its capabilities, like the training of an athlete, and allow him or her to learn and repeat specific, very precise movements, like the training of a dancer. On another level, the actor is learning to use movement to immediately react spontaneously to any external or imagined stimulus without planning or conscious thought. The ideal state of mind of the actor, according to Grotowski, 'is a passive readiness to realize an active role, a state in which one does not **"want to do that"** but rather **"resigns from not doing it".**'

Plastiques

Each person should work on a different part of the body, such as hand, leg, foot, wrist and so on. Create three different detailed movements for that part of the body and practice them until you can perform them precisely, time after time. Find a partner and teach one another your three moves until you can repeat them with total precision. Do the same with a second partner; you should now know nine very precise movements, three for each of three different parts of the body, and be able to repeat them exactly as you have learned them. Now work with a different partner. Improvise a physical 'dialogue', as in the corporal exercises, between you and your partner using different combinations of the moves you have learned, responding to one another but taking care to maintain the precision of the original movements. Think of an association to go with each move (do not discuss it with your partner or pre-plan it) to give it life and purpose and which fits in with the actions of your partner. Introduce an object and continue your work, responding to both the object and your partner. Although your movements will be very different from those used by Grotowski and his colleagues, you are using them in a very similar way.

Performing these exercises in relation to something or someone else is a crucial part of Grotowski's training—he rejected some yoga exercises because they were too introspective. Grotowski often said that real acting is about *re*acting, and the most basic actions for an actor to perform are watching and listening—genuinely and fully watching and listening, not demonstrating the appearance of doing so. Lisa Wolford, who worked with Grotowski and has written a lot about his work, said:

> If I were asked to convey in a few words the most fundamental aspect of what I learned as Grotowski's student in California or as an observer of the research team in residence at his Italian Workcenter, this would be one of the first things that would come to my mind: the indispensable necessity for the actor to live in relation to something or someone outside the self.

The Actor's Role

Grotowski's theatre focuses very strongly on the art of the actor, and all other elements of theatre are eradicated or minimised, which strengthens the bond between the actor and the spectator. Grotowski said:

> The actor is a man who works in public with his body, offering it publicly. If this body restricts itself to demonstrating what is—something that any average person can do—then it is not an obedient instrument capable of performing a spiritual act.

Grotowski's actors were not there to perform everyday actions that the spectators can do themselves. His references to the actor offering his body publicly and performing a spiritual act compare the actor's art to a religious, public sacrifice, which is precisely what Grotowski wanted from his, as he termed them, holy actors. His theatre did not promote Christianity or any other religion; the actors were trying to perform a spiritual function for the spectators separate from any religious beliefs (Grotowski explained, 'Don't get me wrong. I speak about "holiness" as an unbeliever. I mean a "secular holiness".'). Grotowski said,

> If the actor, by setting himself a challenge publicly challenges others, and through excess, profanation and

outrageous sacrilege reveals himself by casting off his everyday mask, he makes it possible for the spectator to undergo a similar process of self-penetration. If he does not exhibit his body, but annihilates it, burns it, frees it from every resistance to any psychic impulse, then he does not sell his body but sacrifices it.

The function of the actor, therefore, is to force the spectator to examine himself or herself by exposing, or 'sacrificing', the deepest parts of the actor's own psyche, including 'the most painful, that which is not intended for the eyes of the world'. This requires absolute commitment from the actors as they will be showing parts of their inner selves that most people are unable to show; it also requires a body trained to project these deepest thoughts and feelings truthfully and completely without blocking their communication to an audience.

The above quotation, while describing Grotowski's ideal actor, also hints at the type of acting he despised. Grotowski likened the type of acting that tries hard to please the audience and responds to audience reaction instead of inner impulses to prostitution, and labelled the actor who practised it a 'courtesan actor'. He said, 'The difference between the "courtesan actor" and the "holy actor" is the same as the difference between the skill of a courtesan and the attitude of giving and receiving which springs from true love: in other words, self-sacrifice.' There does appear to be a paradox here, in that the actor must be aware of his audience and connect with it on a profound level, but must also avoid playing to it or responding to its reactions. These opposing requirements were not, in Grotowski's view, irreconcilable.

If the actor is there to expose his own personality, what about the character he is playing?

The actor in Grotowski's theatre is not there to pretend to be someone else. Whilst Ryszard Cieslak played the title role in Calderon's *The Constant Prince* and Zbigniew Cynkutis portrayed Marlowe's *Dr Faustus*, there was no process of discovering a part from Given Circumstances as with

Stanislavski's techniques or of building up a character using mannerisms, gestures, make-up and costume. The character is a tool to examine the actor's own self and to expose this to an audience. On the other hand, the character is necessary in order to provide a rigid framework for this exploration of self to take place. Grotowski said,

> [The actor] must learn to use his role as if it were a surgeon's scalpel, to dissect himself ... The important thing is to use the role as a trampolin, an instrument with which to study what is hidden behind our everyday mask—the innermost core of our personality—in order to sacrifice it, expose it.

The purpose of this exposure of the actor's self is to provoke the spectator into undertaking a similar self-analysis, which the spectator may resist, as: 'We try to escape the truth about ourselves, whereas here we are invited to stop and take a closer look.' For the spectators, the experience should be therapeutic, purging their emotions and giving them a greater self-knowledge, similar to the idea of catharsis in ancient Greek theatre. An actor's performance is therefore very personal to him or her, and there can be no definitive, objective portrayal of any character as each actor will bring something different to the role. Grotowski said:

> Professors will tell us, each for himself, that they have discovered an objective Hamlet. They suggest to us revolutionary Hamlets, rebel and impotent Hamlets, Hamlet the outsider, etc. But there is no objective Hamlet. The work is too great for that ... My encounter with the text resembles my encounter with the actor and his with me.

There are dangers with destroying these psychological masks; they are our method of interfacing with the real world, of putting over a particular image of our self and of hiding much of our emotional baggage, often from ourselves as much as from others. To drop this barrier and expose ourselves to psychological scrutiny can be traumatic and can even cause lasting emotional damage. Grotowski said that confusion and damage could only be caused if the actor enters into the process half-heartedly, and if he gives himself totally to the work he will become more complete as a person and be able to replace his everyday mask with full knowledge of why it is there and what it is hiding. Spectators, too, can enter into the process fully or leave their barriers raised, in which case they are likely to leave the performance more confused than when they came. However even for the resistant spectator, Grotowski believed that 'the performance represents a form of social psycho-therapy, whereas for the actor it is only a therapy if he has given himself whole-heartedly to his task'. The performances of the Poor Theatre were not staged for the spectator who goes to the theatre 'to have something to talk about to his friends and to be able to say that he has seen this or that play and it was interesting' or 'the man who goes to the theatre to relax after a hard day's work' but 'the spectator who has genuine spiritual needs and who really wishes, through confrontation with the performance, to analyse himself'.

Grotowski accepted that the ideal of a holy actor was something to strive towards but could never be achieved perfectly due to natural limitations and barriers. However this did not mean that the work was futile. He said,

> I think it is just as well founded as that of movement at the speed of light. By this I mean that without ever attaining it, we can nevertheless move consciously and systematically in that direction thus achieving practical results.

Text

Grotowski often spoke against the primacy of the play text in most theatre productions, but his own productions were all based to some extent on pre-existing texts. He complained that, 'In France, plays published in book form are given the title of **Theatre**—a mistake in my opinion, because this is not theatre but dramatic literature.' He described two methods of creating theatre from dramatic literature, neither of which he believed was satisfactory: using the actors and the performance to illustrate the text, 'In that case, the result is not theatre, and the only living element in such a performance is the literature'; or ignoring the text almost completely, 'treating it solely as a pretext, making interpolations and changes, reducing it to nothing'. Some of Grotowski's own productions may appear to fall into this second category, but he believed that his task as a director and artist was not to be a slave to the text on the page, nor to ignore it and create something that had little to do with the playwright's work. Grotowski described the text of a play as having 'the same function as the myth had for the poet of ancient times'. By this he meant that when writers such as Sophocles and Aeschylus wrote plays based on great myths, they did not simply reproduce known stories in a dramatic form but used them as a framework to create theatre that reflected the writers' own experiences, views and personalities. He said, 'The author of **Prometheus** found in the Prometheus myth both an act of defiance and a spring-board, perhaps even the source of his own creation. But his **Prometheus** was the product of his personal experience.'

For a director to work with a play on such a personal level, there must be something in its content that he or she can relate to. Grotowski describes his work on a play as an 'encounter', which 'proceeds from a fascination' and asserts that every director 'must seek encounters which suit his own nature'. The works that fascinated him, such as those by Marlowe and Calderon and the Polish romantic poets, highlighted a strong confrontation between experiences and beliefs of people in the past and our own experiences and prejudices. Marlowe was writing *Dr Faustus* for a sixteenth century London audience and could not have foreseen how it could be relevant to a twentieth-century Polish audience, but Grotowski brought his own experiences to the play to relate it to the lives of his spectators. He believed that an audience would go to see a play from hundreds or even thousands of years ago not merely to observe how people from that time lived ('Perhaps, yes—but that's a job for the professors') but because there are parallels between their lives and ours. The differences in the way these issues are presented and dealt with actually help us to look at them in a different way. As Grotowski put it, 'The characters of the **Odyssey** are still actual because there are still pilgrims. We too are pilgrims. Their pilgrimage is different from ours, and it is for this reason that it throws a new light on our condition.'

A textual encounter

Think of a story from a play, poem, novel, short story, myth or religious text that was not written recently, where some aspect of that story has fascinated you or connected with you in some way. Perhaps you were interested in the way Macbeth or Richard will stop at nothing to gain and hang on to power; maybe Dr Faustus's desperate thirst for knowledge of the world, whatever the cost of acquiring it, has special resonance for you; maybe the extreme acts of Medea against her own children keep coming back to haunt you. According to Grotowski, the root of that fascination probably lies with a connection between the concerns and feelings of the characters in the story and your own, however far removed their world is from yours. Look for what aspects of the story you can relate to and think about when you have felt the same—perhaps not as intensely—as the characters in the story, then improvise with others some scenes that bring out these aspects. You are not writing a literary adaptation and you are not trying to transfer the play to a modern setting such as putting *Romeo and Juliet* into an Ibiza night club or *King Lear* into the board room of a multi-national company (in any case, Grotowski believed that the historical setting actually helped to highlight the common areas of concern). Within the rigid framework of the original story, you are finding within yourself feelings of your own that you can channel through the feelings of the characters in the play in order to give them greater intensity and authenticity. Remember that a Grotowski performance is based around encounters between characters, not solitary expressions of feelings.

Performance space

For his 1961 production of Mickiewicz's *Forefather's Eve*, Grotowski removed the rows of seats facing the stage and instead seated the spectators in small, scattered groups, and his actors performed amongst them. The physical separation of actors and audience had gone, allowing the spectators to become much more involved in the performance. After this, the basic design of each production had to address the issue of creating a specific actor—audience relationship, but this was not simply a case of mixing performers and spectators in the same area; each production assigned the spectators a different role appropriate to the play. In Grotowski's production of Slowacki's *Kordian*, spectators sat on hospital beds cast in the roles of inmates and doctors of the asylum. Actors spoke directly to spectators and asked them questions, but it was found that spectators were unable to lower their daily masks and be spontaneous and so it did not work. The problem, according to Grotowski, was that, 'we ignored the obvious fact that the spectators are anyway playing the role of spectators—they are observers! And when we put them in the role of madmen we simply disturbed their natural function as observers—or, in the best case—as witnesses; in consequence their reactions were not natural.'

For Marlowe's *Dr Faustus*, the spectators were again given a role, but one that allowed them to participate as observers. They were sat at long tables as invited guests in Faustus's banqueting hall, and Faustus told them his story and showed them flashbacks to illustrate his tale. He could address them directly and make eye contact with individuals without waiting for a verbal response, but the spectators could respond as an audience with looks, silences, changes in their breathing and varying levels of attention. While they were playing an actual role within the scene, nothing was expected of them except to react naturally to what they saw and heard. Grotowski said,

> If the spectator and the actor are very close in the space, a strong psychic curtain falls between them. It's the opposite of what one might expect. But if the spectators

play the role of spectators and that role has a function within the production, the psychic curtain vanishes.

In Grotowski's production of Calderon's *Constant Prince*, the spectators were completely separated from the audience as they looked down on the action over a wall from an elevated position, 'as medical students observe an operation, a surgery'. He considered that the extreme and constant psychophysical level of Ryszard Cieslak's performance would be too uncomfortable for the audience to bear if it had too close a relationship with the action, so they observed from a position almost totally hidden from the actors' view to analyse the actions of the characters as in a scientific experiment. This may seem to contradict his ideas on the actor—audience relationship, but Grotowski disagreed:

> Some of my foreign students were deceived. They said, 'You are a traitor to the idea of osmosis between the spectator and the actor.' I am always ready to be a traitor to any exclusive rule. It is not essential that actors and spectators be mixed. The important thing is that the relation between the actors and the spectators in space be a significant one.

The actor and the spectator

Take a play that you know well—perhaps the one you used for the exercise *A textual encounter*. Decide on a single stage setting that can incorporate everything you intend to show to your audience, and then think of a role that your spectators can play in that setting that does not require them to change their role as observers. For instance, you may want to focus *Hamlet* around the royal court and have your spectators as courtiers, or your audience for *Oedipus the King* may consist of citizens of Thebes, or perhaps they pass judgment on the private plottings of the Macbeths from where they cannot be seen by the characters. Your spectators must have a role that justifies them being in the scene but which does not require them to do anything other than observe. Your actors should work out their relationship with the spectators-in-role as they would with any other character in the play in order to communicate with them in the right way. If you can, stage a short section of your play for a small audience.

Sample Questions

1. In what ways do you believe Grotowski's work was influenced by:
   a. Artaud
   b. Stanislavski
2. Describe Grotowski's ideas about the relationship between the actor and the spectator. Illustrate this by showing how you would stage any play you know well using Grotowski's techniques.

6 Peter Brook

Biography Overview

Peter Stephen Paul Brook was born on 21 March 1925 in London to Latvian parents who had escaped from Belgium just before it was invaded by Germany. His mother was a doctor of science and his father a pharmaceutical manufacturer. Brook was fascinated by theatre and films from an early age, and he directed a four-hour production of *Hamlet* on a toy stage at the age of seven. His parents wanted him to be a lawyer, but at the age of sixteen he announced to his father that he was leaving school to work in the movies. His father told him he could see what it was like provided that he went to university after a year. He worked for a year for the Crown Film Unit, and then in 1942 he began a degree in English literature and foreign languages at Magdalen College, Oxford, where he founded the Oxford University Film Society.

He directed a production of Marlowe's *Dr Faustus* at the Torch Theatre in London in 1942, and the following year he made his first film, of Laurence Stern's *A Sentimental Journey through France and Italy*, with a group of undergraduate friends. After leaving Oxford in 1944 he worked for a London film studio making commercial and propaganda films, and continued to direct in small theatres. He received favourable reviews for his production of Cocteau's *Infernal Machine* at the Chanticleer Theatre in South Kensington, and went on to work for Kew Theatre and to direct Shaw's *Pygmalion* for ENSA, the entertainments organisation of the British armed forces. This last production directly led to him being invited to direct Paul Scofield in Shaw's *Man and Superman* at Birmingham Repertory Theatre in August 1945. In 1946, he became the youngest ever director for the Stratford-upon-Avon Festival with his production of *Love's Labours Lost* at the Shakespeare Memorial Theatre.

He worked for a few London companies after this, but then returned to Stratford in 1947 to direct *Romeo and Juliet* on a bare, orange stage with stark white lighting and drastic cuts to the text. This simplicity of design was not what audiences of Shakespeare expected at the time; the Coventry Evening Telegraph complained, 'While nobody minds the brilliant Mr Brook bedevilling lesser plays, I suggest he might be more modest with masterpieces.'

In 1949, when he was still only twenty-four, Brook was appointed Director of Productions at Covent Garden where he directed a number of opera productions. He also continued to direct films, including the 1955 film of John Gay's *The Beggar's Opera* starring Laurence Olivier, and the occasional Stratford stage production, including Laurence Olivier and Vivien Leigh in *Titus Andronicus* in 1955 and John Gielgud in *The Tempest* in 1957. In 1962, Brook completed his film of William Golding's novel *Lord of the Flies* with a cast of children and returned to Stratford to direct Paul Scofield in *King Lear* (this was made into a film which was released in Britain in 1971). This was his first production for the newly formed Royal Shakespeare Company; Peter Hall had invited him to run the company together with himself and Michel Saint-Denis and Brook accepted on the condition that he could have his own experimental group within the company. Hall agreed, and Brook conducted experimental work with a small group of actors under the Artaud-influenced title *Theatre of Cruelty*. These experiments were given a public showing at the LAMDA (London Academy of Music and Dramatic Art) Theatre Studio in March 1963, and then again with different material in early 1964, which received a mixed reception. However they were intended to test their ideas in front of an audience and were not complete, polished productions for the general public.

Brook's group went on to create productions of Peter Weiss's *The Persecution and Assassination of Jean-Paul Marat as Performed by the Inmates of the Asylum of Charenton under the Direction of the Marquis de Sade*—usually shortened to *Marat-Sade*—in 1964, which became one of Brook's most famous and influential productions, and *US* in 1966.

Marat-Sade is a play-within-a-play in which the Marquis de Sade, confined to Charenton by Napoleon, puts on his own play about the French Revolution using inmates of the asylum as his actors. The performance required Brook's actors to simulate some extremes of insane behaviour, which was exhausting and often frightening for them. *US* was a reaction to the Vietnam war and was put together by the company in four months, including two weeks of exercises led by Jerzy Grotowski whom Brook had brought to England to help with the production. It opened at the Aldwych Theatre in London in October 1966. The first half consisted of documentary material about the war acted out in various different styles, interspersed with poems by Adrian Mitchell. Most of the second half was a dialogue between a man about to commit suicide and a girl whose liberal views are gradually broken down. The performance ended with a box of butterflies being released over the audience, one of which was burned on stage (it was a fake, but was made to look very real). In 1966, nothing like *US* had been performed in the theatre before, certainly in the UK, but 'documentary theatre' became a popular style that is still seen in theatre today.

Brook gave a series of lectures in 1968 at the Universities of Hull, Keele, Manchester and Sheffield that were published as The Empty Space, which is still essential reading for anyone studying or creating theatre. In August 1970, his production of *A Midsummer Night's Dream* opened in Stratford before playing a season at the Aldwych and then touring the United States. This has become one of the most famous productions of Shakespeare of the twentieth century, drawing such praise from critics as, 'more than refreshing, magnificent, the sort of thing one sees only once in a generation, and then only from a man of genius' (Harold Hobson, *The Sunday Times*) and 'without any equivocation whatsoever the greatest production of Shakespeare I have ever seen in my life' (Clive Barnes, *The Observer Magazine*). Designer Sally Jacobs created a plain white box to enclose the play with a gallery running along the top of it from which actors would observe the action when they were not actively involved in a scene. Ladders, swings, ropes and trapezes were hung around the

115

stage, and the actors demonstrated some impressive physical skills such as juggling, stilt walking, tumbling, trapeze work and plate spinning. The play is filled with magic, and this production created its magical effects using only the abilities of its performers rather than stage effects. With this impressive and original production, Brook bid his farewell not only to the RSC but also to Britain.

In 1970, Brook moved to France where he set up the International Centre for Theatre Research (CIRT— Centre International de Recherche Théâtrale, later to be renamed the CICT—Centre International de Création Théâtrales). He had been granted sufficient funding to remove the constraints of commercial theatre that he believed throttled the artistic process. Brook put together a company of actors from different parts of the world with very different cultural backgrounds, methods of training and approaches to performance. The first production from this group was *Orghast* in 1971 that reworked the Prometheus myth, for which poet Ted Hughes invented a new language that used the music and rhythm of verbal utterances and the power of incantation to communicate. In December 1972, Brook took his actors on an 8500-mile trek around Africa, during which they stopped and performed for any groups of people they encountered, experimenting with different types of stories and methods of performance to try to gain a positive reception and understanding from their spectators.

In 1974, the company moved into the run-down nineteenth century theatre the Bouffes du Nord on the outskirts of Paris, which was built in 1874 but had been empty since 1952. This faded, once grand building became the backdrop to his subsequent productions, beginning with *Timon d'Athènes* in 1974 with a French text adapted from Shakespeare's play by one of Brook's main collaborators, Jean-Claude Carrière. Brook continued to find inspiration in Shakespeare, but the company's work also included such diverse productions as *The Conference of the Birds* in 1979 based on a twelfth century Sufi poem and an adaptation of Bizet's *Carmen* entitled *La Tragédie de Carmen* in 1981. Another of Brook's major theatrical landmarks appeared in its original French version in 1985: *The Mahabharata*. This nine-hour production was based on the epic Sanskrit poem of the same name that forms the heart of Hindu mythology. This production toured the world and was later filmed for television.

Brook and his company have continued to produce fresh new work and fresh productions of older works, particularly Shakespeare. In 1993, his company created *L'Homme Qui* (*The Man Who*), based on the real-life case studies of psychologist Oliver Sacks in his book *The Man Who Mistook His Wife For A Hat*. In December 2000, his *Hamlet* with British actor Adrian Lester in the title role made a big impact on Paris audiences, and did the same in London when it opened at the Young Vic in August 2001. As he approaches his eightieth year, Brook shows little sign of wanting to retire.

Theory and Practice

The empty space

I can take any empty space and call it a bare stage. A man walks across this empty space whilst someone else is watching him, and this is all that is needed for an act of theatre to be engaged.

This is the opening of Brook's famous 1968 book on theatre *The Empty Space*. When Brook started to direct Shakespeare in Stratford, he avoided conventions in acting, speaking, design and staging that many people believed were indispensable elements of Shakespearean productions, if not of theatre as a whole, and later did the same in his opera productions. His breaks with tradition were not popular with everyone, but he believed it was important to move away from defining *theatre* as 'a theatre of box office, foyer, tip-up seats, footlights, scene changes, intervals, music, as though the theatre was by very definition these and little more'. Whilst theatre can contain all of these, the essential elements of a theatrical performance are a performer doing something in a space and a spectator watching him. This concept is at the heart of all of Brook's theatre making it, like

Grotowski's theatre, an actor's theatre, whether the company is performing Chekhov in London or New York or a fable about magic shoes on a piece of carpet in the Sahara desert to some passing nomads. John Heilpern, wrote,

> Brook's form of theatre is said to be a director's theatre. But it isn't. It is an actor's theatre, for the actor alone conjures up the magic. But it is also an audience's theatre. For the one holds up the silk scarf, and the other imagines the newborn child.

Heilpern was with Brook's company on the African journey, and he documented the experience in his book *Conference of the Birds*. In this he wrote,

> Brook, perceived as the intellectual figure of theatre, is in practice the reverse. He is about accessibility. He wants to make theatre, whatever the complexity of the material, accessible to the widest human response without watering anything down. That's what is great about Brook: he trusts audiences.

This trust means that he will put complex material before a general audience without feeling the need to simplify or 'dumb down' in order for it to be understood. He admired the renaissance theatre, where a mixed audience from a very broad range of social and educational backgrounds gathered together in the same building to watch a popular but intelligent form of theatre from writers like William Shakespeare. Brook also trusts his audiences to complete the picture suggested by his performers; he does not feel he has to spell everything out for them to understand and leaves them to use their imaginations to fill in the gaps. The actor holds up the silk scarf, and the spectator imagines the newborn child.

Communication

The following is based on exercises performed by Brook's actors during the *Theatre of Cruelty* experiments at the Royal Shakespeare Company.

i. Position one person—the actor—in front of the rest of the group—the spectators. The actor imagines a dramatic situation that does not involve any movement and the spectators try to work out what is in the actor's mind (or as Brook puts it 'understand what state he is in').

ii. It probably won't take you too long to come to the conclusion that this is impossible. Now the actor should try to find the very least that he or she needs to do in order to communicate with the spectators. This could be a sound or a movement or any method of communication you can think of. Experiment with different methods to find the most effective one to achieve understanding.

iii. An actor (take it in turns) must communicate an idea to spectators but with no words and by only using:
    a. one finger
    b. a cry
    c. a whistle
    d. eyes and eyelids

iv. One person sits at one end of the room facing the wall and a second person is positioned at the other end facing the first person's back. The second person must make the first obey his or her commands, but only sounds are allowed, not words (and coded sounds cannot be agreed in advance). This may sound impossible, but with perseverance and concentration this can work. Brook reported that they often observed 'a long silence, one actor running experimentally through a range of hisses or gurgles until suddenly the other actor stood and quite confidently executed the movement the first one had in mind'.

v. In pairs, experiment with different ways of communicating something to your partner. One person should have something in mind that they really need to communicate to their partner, but they can only use the simple method that they have agreed on. This could be movement of the eyes only, tapping the finger nail on a table, moaning, movement of just the fingers and so on.

In each of these exercises, an action (which could be a movement or a sound) always comes from a thought or idea (Grotowski called it an impulse) and a desire to communicate that to someone else. The actor does not perform any action that does not go towards communicating that idea.

Although this form of communication relies on the most basic of actions, people with similar cultural backgrounds, even if they speak different languages, can use shortcut signs that people from different cultures may not understand or may interpret differently. For instance, a 'wolf whistle' indicates to those who understand it that you find someone attractive; a wink of one eye indicates a friendly greeting or a confidential understanding shared with someone. Those same signs may mean something different or nothing at all if they are used to try to communicate to someone from a remote African tribe or a nomad living in the Sahara.

In his search for a universal form of human communication that transcends these cultural signs, Brook put together a group of performers from different parts of the world, each of whom brought to the group their own culture, background and methods of working. He then took this group to perform to audiences that shared nothing with them in terms of language or culture and tried to create performances that they could all understand and relate to. It was found that the same performance could provoke very different reactions from different audiences with no obvious explanation. For instance, a play called *The Shoe Show* about a pair of magic shoes that could transform the wearer into someone else was loved by the Tuaregs in the Sahara but hated by villagers in Nigeria. The actors could not fall back on western theatrical conventions because they would not be understood. In a village in Africa where the local Hausa language does not even have a word for "theatre", it was found that a young actor could not play an old man by clichéd actions such as stooping and coughing because the villagers would simply see a young stranger stooping and coughing, not an old man. Heilpern concludes his telling of this story with:

> So he must begin again. He must stop 'acting'. And if he can find something fresh and extraordinary within him, he will convince any audience in the world of something very rare: a universal emotional truth. And then the theatre can become irresistible—a completely truthful, natural event.

That's Brook's achievement, I think.

Cross-cultural communication

i. You (the performer) are being visited by a group of intelligent creatures from Mars (the audience) who happen to have learned perfect English but know nothing of Earth customs or culture. They want you to explain what some objects are and what they are used for. However if you mention anything else in your explanation that they have not come across you will have to explain this as well. Take it in turns to be the performer, while everyone else is the Martian audience who should ask for clarification of anything they do not understand. Examples of the sorts of things they want to learn about are:

a. a hammer

b. books

c. the telephone

d. a water tap

e. a bicycle

f. curtains

g. a clock

h. a plate

ii. Once you have entertained the Martian party, you are visited by a group of people from Venus. The Venutian party are just as intelligent as the Martians, but they have not learned any Earth languages. You must therefore act out the objects and their use for them to understand. If there is anything they find confusing, they will respond with the confused beeps and whistles familiar to anyone with knowledge of Venutian languages.

iii. Now you have gained a reputation for interplanetary relations, you are sent to a remote part of Jupiter to visit a tribe of people who have no verbal language and who have not discovered space travel so they know nothing of other planets or their inhabitants. You wish to tell them the story of your journey to see them, but you have no way of explaining to them even that you are acting out a story. Get together a small group of actors and, using only your body and sounds (not words), prepare your audience for what you are about to do and act out your story for them. If you get a favourable reaction, you may wish to try acting out other stories.

Of course these experiments are entirely artificial, and you will have to agree on a level of knowledge that your spectators have in order to get anywhere at all. Brook's experiments were with real people who reacted immediately to the performance to show whether it was understood and appreciated.

The four theatres

In *The Empty Space*, Brook describes four categories of theatre: Deadly, Holy, Rough and Immediate; these may exist in the same town or city or hundreds of miles apart, or more than one may be combined in a single theatre or even a single play.

The Deadly Theatre

Deadly Theatre is, quite simply, bad theatre, and is, according to Brook in 1968, the theatre we see most often. It would be easy to stick the Deadly label just on popular, commercial theatre, but Brook warns us that 'it is not just the trivial comedy and the bad musical that fail to give us our money's worth—the Deadly Theatre finds its deadly way into grand opera and tragedy, into the plays of Molière and the plays of Brecht' and 'The Deadly Theatre takes easily to Shakespeare.' We may go to a production of a Shakespeare play that includes all the ingredients we expect from classical theatre, 'Yet secretly we find it excruciatingly boring—and in our hearts we either blame Shakespeare, or theatre as such, or even ourselves.' Actors and directors base their performances, perhaps not always consciously, on ideas and images from older productions and academic studies instead of looking anew at the text and trying to bring it to life for a contemporary audience. Some younger actors, in a search for what they believe to be 'truth' in their acting, try to deliver their dialogue in a more naturalistic, everyday-speech style, but the formal verse structure does not adapt easily to such a delivery and gives the appearance of weak acting and unintelligible speech.

Reciting the text

This is an exercise that Brook tried at a lecture with a woman in his audience who had not seen or read *King Lear*. The following is Goneril's first speech from this play, spoken to her father, the King:

> Sir, I love you more than words can wield the matter;
> Dearer than eyesight, space, and liberty;
> Beyond that can be valued, rich or rare;
> No less than life, with grace, health, beauty, honour;
> As much as child e'er loved, or father found;
> A love that makes breath poor, and speech unable;
> Beyond all manner of so much I love you.

  i. Recite this text out loud, ignoring anything you may know about the play or the character.

  ii. Now read the text again, but load it with hypocrisy, as though said by a wicked woman who will state her love for her father in public and then plot behind his back in secret.

The second is an example of what Brook called 'acting to a definition', in other words trying to act 'wickedness'

> instead of playing the text. The verse works when spoken by a fine lady in a public expression of her love for her father and her King, but when the extra layer—which is not suggested by anything in the speech—is added it becomes awkward and false. If the scene is played as simply as the words suggest, the balance of the whole play is changed, becoming a more complex and less crude journey for the characters and the audience.

Brook wrote:

> In a living theatre, we would each day approach the rehearsal putting yesterday's discoveries to the test, ready to believe that the true play has once again escaped us. But the Deadly Theatre approaches the classics from the viewpoint that somewhere, someone has found out and defined how the play should be done.

If the theatre is so bad, why do people go and watch it?

Brook wrote in 1968 that people were stopping going to the theatre because it is deadly and expensive. However the relationship between audience numbers and deadliness or artistry of the productions is not a simple one. There are many elements that conspire together to keep the Deadly Theatre going.

Audiences. Odd as it may seem, audiences are as much the cause as they are the victims of Deadly Theatre. Some people associate 'culture' with something rather dull in historical costumes with long speeches, and so if they see something that they find, if they are honest, a little boring and difficult to understand they believe the event must have been worthwhile and 'good' for them. These Deadly Spectators make dull productions into successes, and therefore they continue to be produced. Brook explained:

> Audiences crave for something in the theatre that they can term 'better' than life and for this reason are open to confuse culture, or the trappings of culture, with something they do not know, but sense obscurely could

exist—so, tragically, in elevating something bad into a success they are only cheating themselves.

Actors. Brook does not blame actors for deadliness in their acting, and in fact he sympathises with their predicament. Actors often have little real control over a production and a very short rehearsal time to perfect their performance. Their craft is also viewed very differently to other performance arts, as singers and dancers will usually retain the services of a teacher for the whole of their careers, whereas an actor has a short period of training and then is given no assistance to develop.

Critics. The critic has an uneasy association with the theatre and is often blamed for closing shows by putting audiences off going to see them. Brook recounts a story of one of his productions in Paris that had been savaged by the press critics and was, as a result, playing to nearly empty houses. He announced three free performances, and audiences fought to get in and loved the production. However, he believes that critics are essential to maintaining a healthy theatre, even if they may not always perform this function particularly well and are often reduced to tipsters, giving star ratings for people who want to decide what to see at a glance. According to Brook, 'a critic is always serving the theatre when he is hounding out incompetence'. In addition to 'calling for competence', 'He is a pathmaker.' By this, Brook means that the critic should be helping theatre to move towards a 'less deadly, but, as yet, largely undefined theatre.' Critic and artist should both have the same goal: to work towards an ideal theatre, but to be constantly revising their definitions of what that ideal theatre is.

Playwrights. Brook believes that 'It is woefully difficult to write a play', but he does not believe that most playwrights successfully achieve even their own aims and that 'too few authors are what we could truly call inspiring or inspired'. Few writers are able, in Brook's view, to combine the outside world with the inner world of the characters in a way that Shakespeare did four hundred years ago. One of the problems was that conventional play forms were no longer relevant to audiences, and so a writer must either 'begin at the root—by facing the problem of the very nature of dramatic utterance' or 'settle for a second-hand vehicle that's no longer in working order and very unlikely to take him to where he wants to go'.

Directors. The problem of form is the same for a director as for a writer: 'the deadly director uses old formulae, old methods, old jokes, old effects, stock beginnings to scenes, stock ends'. To avoid this, the director must have the confidence to begin each production with nothing and to find the production from within the play's text and not from old ideas and productions.

The Holy Theatre

Brook called his second category Holy Theatre, but it has no direct connection with religion. His alternative title is The Theatre of the Invisible-Made-Visible, because it uses concrete images and sounds to suggest or symbolise abstract themes and ideas to the audience. Something abstract such as an emotion or an idea cannot be put on stage; it must be represented by something concrete such as words, images, actions or sounds. Brook gave an example of this: 'we recognize that a magical thing called music can come from men in white ties and tails, blowing, waving, thumping and scraping away ... ordinary men and their clumsy instruments are transformed by an act of possession'. This music is then absorbed by the conductor, and 'if he is relaxed, open and attuned, then the invisible will take possession of him; through him, it will reach us'. Note Brook's use of terminology that suggests religion, spirituality and magic such as 'magical', 'transformed', 'act of possession' and 'the invisible'.

Making the invisible visible

Try to represent each of the following themes using: words (dialogue); an action; an image; a sound.

   i. Love
  ii. Fear

---

iii. Hope
iv. Oppression
v. Knowledge
vi. Prejudice
vii. Magic
viii. Beauty
ix. Sacrifice
x. Holy

Brook notes that most forms of theatre have their origins in religious ceremonies, but the ritual elements of theatre have all but disappeared: 'Even if theatre had in its origins rituals that made the invisible incarnate, we must not forget that apart from certain Oriental theatres these rituals have been either lost or remain in seedy decay.' The theatres of ancient Greece staged plays as part of a religious festival that were said to be of spiritual benefit to the spectators. Greek theatre is the model that most Western theatre is based on, but 'Over the centuries the Orphic Rites turned into the Gala Performance—slowly and imperceptibly the wine was adulterated drop by drop.' However the desire for rituals and the feeling that they should exist in our lives does not go away. Some artists, attempting to fill this need, try to create new rituals modelled on those of ancient cultures, but the results are usually superficial constructions of the outer forms of ceremonies without any roots or relevance in society.

Brook's concept of Holy Theatre is greatly inspired by Artaud and Grotowski. Brook said of Artaud:

> ... he wanted a theatre that would be a hallowed place; he wanted that theatre served by a band of dedicated actors and directors who would create out of their own natures an unending succession of violent stage images ... He wanted an audience that would drop all of its defences, that would allow itself to be perforated, shocked, startled, and raped, so that at the same time it could be filled with a powerful new charge.

127

When he talks about Grotowski, he talks of the Grotowski actor revealing himself—he uses the word 'sacrifice' as Grotowski did—as a service to the spectators, and likens the relationship between actor and spectator in the Holy Theatre with that between a priest and a worshipper. The Holy Theatre does not serve any organised religion; it tries to provide the same service to its spectators as religious ritual once did before, as many believe, these rituals became mechanical, lifeless and meaningless to most people. Brook said, 'This theatre is holy because its purpose is holy; it has a clearly defined place in the community and it responds to a need the churches can no longer fill.' Artaud investigated the rituals of ancient cultures during his trip to Mexico to try to create new rituals for his own culture that could be shared using theatre. Grotowski's actors have given up everything so that their work has become their way of life like a priest, and their performance is an act of sacrifice, revealing parts of themselves that most of us keep hidden in order to persuade the spectators to examine their own selves; 'The priest performs the ritual for himself and on behalf of others.'

Theatre and religion

List as many similarities you can think of between:

- Theatre buildings and places of worship.
- Theatre performances and religious ceremonies.
- Acting in the theatre and conducting a religious service.
- Watching a performance in the theatre and attending a religious service.

Religions all teach that the invisible is there all the time, but to be able to see it requires the observer to be in a particular state or to have achieved a certain level of understanding; this can take a lifetime of study, contemplation and commitment, but holy art, including Holy Theatre, can be of help with this: 'A holy theatre not only presents the invisible but also offers conditions that makes its perception possible.' Brook concludes about Holy Theatre,

In the theatre, the tendency for centuries has been to put the actor at a remote distance, on a platform, framed, decorated, lit, painted, in high shoes—so as to help to persuade the ignorant that he is holy, that his art is sacred. ...Today we have exposed the sham. But we are rediscovering that a holy theatre is still what we need. So where should we look for it? In the clouds or on the ground?

The Rough Theatre

The Rough Theatre is the popular theatre, 'the theatre that's not in a theatre, the theatre on carts, on wagons, on trestles, audiences standing, drinking, sitting round tables, audiences joining in, answering back; theatre in back rooms, upstairs rooms, barns, the one-night stands, the torn sheet pinned across the hall, the battered screen to conceal the quick changes'. This is a theatre that does not need a specially designed theatre space, and instead of striving for unity of design in its set, props and costumes uses whatever is available, so 'a bucket will be banged for a battle, flour used to show faces white with fear'. The result is not something simplistic and 'dumbed down' but a highly sophisticated blend of performance styles from broad comedy to mime to realistic dialogue to stock characters. A popular audience unaware of theatrical conventions accepts inconsistencies in style that an audience of regular theatregoers may find strange or even incomprehensible.

Staging Rough Theatre

Create two boxes: a props box and a costumes box. The props box should contain a random collection of objects of all kinds, but nothing that has been made specifically as a theatre prop. The costume box should contain a variety of jackets, coats, hats, shirts, skirts and so on.

- Each person takes one item from each box and thinks about what character and action the two objects suggest to them. In pairs or small groups, create scenes using these characters and items.

- In groups, each group should choose a popular fairy tale. Stage the story as thoroughly as possible using objects from the two boxes. The objects do not have to be used as what they are; their role in the story should be made clear by how they are used. Costume can also be used simply to show that an actor is now a different character or a narrator when playing multiple roles.
- Take a scene from a Shakespeare play that you know reasonably well. Stage the scene using objects from the two boxes as props and costumes as above. Brook wrote that the most satisfying version of *The Taming of the Shrew* he ever saw avoided any consistency of style and instead let the actors dress in exactly the way they saw the characters; 'I still remember a cowboy, and a fat character busting the buttons of a pageboy's uniform.'

The Rough Theatre is not just rough in its staging; 'filth and vulgarity are natural, obscenity is joyous'. It is also 'anti-authoritarian, anti-traditional, anti-pomp, anti-pretence' and 'it is there unashamedly to make joy and laughter'. It is not ashamed to exploit bodily functions and sexual innuendo for laughs, or to poke fun at politicians, famous people and the law. Brook relates the Rough Theatre to the theatre of Bertolt Brecht, and especially to his concept of alienation, which often used Rough Theatre devices such as placards, popular songs, visible stage lights, vulgar comedy and larger-than-life characters both to entertain and to highlight issues. His other Rough model is Shakespeare and the Elizabethan theatre, where the absence of scenery allowed swift transitions between places, times and even between fantasy and reality as quickly as a cut in cinema or television. Shakespeare's plays combine various styles that seem, on the surface, to be incompatible and resist any attempts to unify them into a single production, but this is deliberate and is pure Rough Theatre. If we look at a play such as *Henry IV* (both parts), we see one scene in formal, regular verse where important matters of state are discussed at court followed by a scene of broad comedy in prose where Falstaff and his friends speak in everyday slang about drinking, sex and robbery. These Rough contrasts, together with the clash of the Rough and the Holy, give Shakespeare's plays a depth and richness that is lost if any attempt is made to unify these disparate elements in a production, because, according to Brook, 'It is through the unreconciled opposition of Rough and Holy, through an atonal screech of absolutely unsympathetic keys that we get the disturbing and the unforgettable impressions of his plays.' Brook wrote:

> Shakespeare is a model of a theatre that contains Brecht and Beckett, but goes beyond both. Our need in the post-Brecht theatre is to find a way forwards, back to Shakespeare.

The Immediate Theatre

Unlike the other three theatres, Brook does not define the Immediate Theatre as something that could be recognised by watching a finished production. It is more a collection of ideas about a theatre that Brook would like to see based on his experiences in creating theatre, and it focuses mostly on the creative process. Naturally it is contrasted with the Deadly Theatre, and the traps at each stage of the process of creating a production that can cause it to fall into deadliness are highlighted.

Theatre is the most immediate art form as it is created now, in the present, before the eyes of the spectators, and when it ends it is gone forever; other arts, including dramatic arts such as film and television, are brought before the public as something already complete. Even during a run of the same production, each performance is created anew each night. However, repetition always carries with it the threat of the deadly if successful elements (moves, gestures, ways of speaking) are simply copied over from previous performances instead of being freshly created each time. This is also true of creating new productions—each element of a production should be questioned and re-examined and not taken for granted, even those that appear to be fundamental such as costume, make-up, lighting and scenery. When the costumes for a new production are considered, the first question is not 'which costumes do we need?' but 'do we need costumes?' Naked actors may produce a reaction from your audience that you do not want, so the answer to this question will probably be 'yes'. Next you need to ask 'why', or what function the costume needs to serve—perhaps to show the character's age, status, occupation, personality or financial status in a naturalistic way, or to illuminate something about the character in a way that has little connection with the realism of the scene, such as the cowboy in *The Taming of the Shrew*.

Back to basics

Take a play that you know well or are working on at the moment. For each of the following elements, ask yourself:

i. Do we need it?

ii. How can we use it to clarify the plot, themes or characters?

- Costume
- Make-up
- Movement
- Music
- Sound
- Scenery
- Props
- Lighting
- Voice

Try to think beyond the obvious, the naturalistic or the traditional; for instance, is it necessary to portray the witches in *Macbeth* with pointed hats and cracked voices?

Brook looks at a number of specific areas of a production and debates how they can be best utilised.

The designer: 'The best designer evolves step by step with the director, going back, changing, scrapping, as a conception of the whole gradually takes form.' It is rarely possible for the design to evolve during rehearsals for practical reasons as the scenery may not be completed by opening night. However the design should be an integral part of the production and not a backdrop against which it takes place. Brook says that he has sometimes settled on a design too early in the process and it has inhibited the development of the production in rehearsals. A designer should produce a picture that is incomplete so that the actors can complete it—'a true theatre designer will think of his designs as being all the time in motion, in action, in relation to what the actor brings to a scene as it unfolds'. The same applies to costume design, which must allow the actor to express everything that he or she has worked on in rehearsals without restriction.

Casting: Every actor has limitations, but typecasting them in similar roles produces the temptation to fall back on tricks and techniques formulated for other productions instead of creating the part afresh. The same actor will work differently amongst different groups of other actors due to differences in technique, age, experience and ability and whether they like one another.

The first rehearsal: 'The first rehearsal is always to a degree the blind leading the blind.' This is the moment that everyone meets and begins working together, and it can be an awkward time both for actors and director. They may talk about the play, look at the designs, read through the play or play games, but this is really all just preparation for the second day, when the work on the play really begins.

The director: The director must learn that rehearsals are a process during which the production will develop at its own pace, and everything must be introduced at the right moment during this process for it to be effective. Too much prior preparation can inhibit this development, and 'the director who comes to the first rehearsal with his script prepared with the moves and business, etc. noted down, is a real deadly theatre man'. To illustrate this, he relates a story of when he was directing *Love's Labours Lost* in Stratford in 1945. The night before the first rehearsal, he worked out every move of every actor for the first entry of the Court using folded cardboard to represent actors on a model of the set and marked everything up in detail in his script. When he tried to translate this to movements of real people on a stage nothing looked right and everyone ended up in the wrong place, but the emerging pattern contained the seeds of something more interesting than the one he had worked out the night before. 'I stopped, and walked away from my book, in amongst the actors, and I have never looked at a written plan since.'

Brook claims that a rotten director can be as effective as a good one, as sheer terror of the audience on the opening night will force the actors to pull together and make something of the production. A plausible, articulate director may persuade an actor to trust the director's vision even if the actor does not feel comfortable with it. If a director is frightened of being seen as a despot and therefore intervenes very little, the group will lack leadership and be unable to create a coherent production. 'At best a director enables an actor to reveal his own performance, that he might otherwise have clouded for himself.'

Sample Questions

1. In what ways do you think Brook's work has been influenced by:
   a. Artaud
   b. Grotowski
2. What elements of Brook's four theatres can you find in the work of:
   a. Artaud
   b. Brecht
   c. Boal
   d. Grotowski
3. Analyse a production you have seen recently to find in it elements of Brook's four theatres.
4. Brook said that Shakespeare's plays combine the Rough with the Holy. Discuss this with reference to at least one play.

7 **Augusto Boal**

Biography Overview

Augusto Pinto Boal was born on 16 March 1931 in Rio de Janeiro, Brazil to Portuguese parents. As a child, he would stage plays with his brothers adapted from romantic novels that his mother received by instalment through the post, and the rest of the family were charged bottle tops to watch them. However he believes that his first actor was his pet goat Chibuco who would perform tricks under Boal's direction; sadly, Chibuco was destined for the dinner table and so his theatrical career was cut short. When he was seventeen, Boal chose to study chemistry at University because his father thought it would lead to a well-paid job (he did not dare to suggest theatre to his father as a subject for serious study or as a future occupation) and because he was very fond of a girl at school who also wanted to do chemistry. Boal passed the entrance examination and went on to study chemistry at the University of Brazil, but the girl did not pass and they were separated.

At University, he put himself forward as Director of the Cultural Department, and, as he was the only candidate for the post, he got it. This gave him access to free tickets for theatre, opera and ballet performances by both Brazilian and foreign companies. He wanted to meet the artists who created these productions to discuss theatre, so he organised a cycle of lectures, and he began by inviting the playwright he most admired, Nelson Rodrigues. The lecture was poorly attended, but Boal struck up a relationship with Rodrigues and through him met other people involved in theatre. He also attended theatre classes at the National Theatre Service purely as an observer rather than a participant, and in 1950 he began searching for a theatre for a company he had set up with theatre students Glaúcio Gil and Leo Jusi called 'O Teatro Artístico do Rio de Janeiro' in imitation of the Moscow

Art Theatre. At first they planned a programme of Russian classics from writers such as Chekhov, Tolstoy, Gorky and Dostoevsky, which they abandoned for Shakespeare, before settling on a more popular repertoire of comedies.

Boal graduated with a degree in chemical engineering in 1952 aged 21, but he needed to study further in order to be a chemical engineer. He travelled to the USA and signed up for playwriting classes with writer John Gassner together with a few other theatre topics, plus classes in chemical engineering, at Columbia University. He became a voluntary reporter for the *Correio Paulistano* and sought people he wanted to meet to interview them. He met a lot of famous people from the theatre, and even spent time as an observer at the Actors' Studio. In 1955 he directed two plays that he had written, *The House Across the Street* and *The Horse and the Saint*, at the Malin Studio, New York with The Writers' Group of Brooklyn, which he had joined the year before.

In July 1955, Boal, now 24, returned to Rio de Janeiro and took a job as a translator for a 'crime, sex and gore' magazine called *X-9*. He often embellished his translations with plot twists of his own creation. The fact that his directorial debut had been on Broadway (at the Malin) impressed people back home, and in 1957 he was offered a job as director at the Teatro de Arena (Theatre in the Round) in São Paulo. He dreamed of directing *Hamlet* on the Arena's tiny stage for his home debut, but John Steinbeck's *Of Mice And Men* had already been scheduled. From his first rehearsal, Boal used Stanislavski as his model as a director, and he claims to have done so ever since. Boal continued to direct for the Arena and he also taught playwriting there in 1958, and then, from 1959, at the Escola de Arte Dramatica in the Seminário de Dramaturgia. The company took productions on tour to out-of-the-way areas in search of audiences from 'the people' or the poor working classes instead of the wealthy middle classes.

Boal had his first serious clash with the authorities with a piece called *L'Engrenage* adapted from a film script written by Jean-Paul Sartre that was never made. The show was to be staged at Ipiranga, but the censors banned it and armed police surrounded the theatre. During a series of playwriting seminars conducted by Boal in the Metalworkers' Trade Union of Santo André, a play written by a worker was performed for other workers, and an early version of the 'spect-actor' (see below) was created by accident; the character of a strike breaker was interrupted by a member of the audience who recognised that the character was based on him, and he took the stage to put forward his own version of events that contradicted the version in the play. In 1964, there was a coup in Brazil, which began twenty years of military dictatorship. The new regime banned trade unions, closed the Centres of Popular Culture and imprisoned people suspected of holding left-wing political views.

Boal's 1965 musical play *Zumbi* introduced the *Sistema Coringa* or Joker System in which the same character could be played by more than one actor at different times so that an actor never 'owned' a single character. The Joker spoke directly to the audience, explained what was happening, made sense of the mixture of messages and performance styles and sometimes played characters in the play. In *Tiradentes* (1967), the lead character was played by a single actor in order to try to regain audience empathy, but the other actors still swapped roles. The Joker again provided the audience with explanations and related the events in the play to events outside the theatre, but he also held interviews with the characters in the middle of the play.

In 1968, Boal directed a collage production at the Arena, a *Feira paulista de opinião* (São Paulo's Fair of Opinions), which combined the work of playwrights, composers and visual artists into a single performance. The censor cut sixty-five pages out of the eighty-page script, but the company decided to perform the entire piece illegally with the full support of Brazil's artistic community. The police surrounded the theatre on the second day, and later surrounded every theatre they tried to perform the play at. They managed to get authorisation from a judge to perform, but the police and the military still tried to sabotage the performances with a combination of attacks and kidnapping. The actors combined their warm-up exercises with target practice in the basement and kept their guns with them at all times while they were on stage for protection.

Richard Schechner of New York University invited Arena to perform *Zumbi* for a week in 1969; this turned into a month of sell-out performances, leading to an invitation to tour the production around Mexico. The following year, Boal began forming Teatro Jornal (Newspaper Theatre) groups made up of ordinary people who were taught how to create their own performances from that morning's newspaper headlines—these performances took place anywhere out of the way of the police. He directed Brecht's *The Resistible Rise of Arturo Ui* at the Arena in 1971 and took *Zumbi* on tour around Argentina, but then he was arrested, imprisoned and tortured. He was registered under a false name at the prison, but his brother Albertino was an army officer and managed to track him down. News of Boal's arrest soon spread and brought demands for his release from important figures in the arts around the world including Peter Brook, Arthur Miller, Richard Schechner, Jean Louis Barrault, Jean Paul Sartre, John Arden, Arianne Mnouchkine and many more; the response of the authorities was to try to convict him as quickly as possible. The judge granted him the right to travel to the Nancy Festival if he signed a document promising to return for sentencing, but the official who made him sign warned him that he would be killed if he did return. He travelled to New York and Europe, then to Buenos Aires in Argentina where he remained for the next five years.

In Argentina, Boal staged a play in a restaurant to publicise a little-known law that gave anyone who was hungry the right to eat for free in any restaurant on showing their identity card, but he did not let his spectators know that they were watching a staged event—his first example of Invisible Theatre. In 1973 in Peru, Forum Theatre was born when Boal could not understand what a spectator was saying to him and invited her on stage to demonstrate what she meant. Image Theatre was created around the same time to solve the problem of his Peruvian students speaking forty-seven different first languages. *O Teatro do Oprimido* (*The Theatre of the Oppressed*), based around the four cornerstones of Newspaper, Invisible, Forum and Image theatres, was published in 1974. He received a bursary from the Guggenheim Foundation and used it to write nine books over the next three years while he waited for a new passport to be granted.

Boal moved to Portugal in 1976 and then, in 1978, to Paris, where he taught Forum Theatre techniques at the Sorbonne and founded the Centre d'Étude et Diffusion des Techniques Active d'Expression (CÉDITADE). He recognised a different form of oppression in Europe; more people were dying in Scandinavia through suicide caused by loneliness and isolation than were being murdered in countries oppressed by dictatorships. This oppression from within he named *Le flic dans la tête*—The cop in the head—and he set up an atelier in Paris in 1982 to work on this idea that lasted for two years.

In 1986, Boal finally returned to Brazil to live (he had visited a few times since the amnesty in 1979) where he joined the Workers' Party and was elected City Councillor. He set up a number of groups to practise Theatre of the Oppressed, and the ideas of ordinary people from these groups were put forward to become law. In four years, thirty bills of law were created using this method and thirteen of them became law. This process became known as Legislative Theatre. He led similar sessions in Legislative Theatre at the local councils of Munich, Paris, London and Bradford.

Boal still talks about his work and teaches his methods all over the world, and his entertaining autobiography, *Hamlet and the Baker's Son*, was published in 2001.

Theory and Practice

Theatre of the Oppressed

'Theatre of the Oppressed' is an overall term for the type of theatre that Boal formulated and practised. His book of the same name traces the origins of a popular theatre part back to ancient Greece and the celebrations of farm labourers after the harvest had been brought in. He argues that the division of theatre into spectators and actors and the dramatic theories of Aristotle in ancient Greece—still extremely influential on modern dramaturgy in theatre, television and cinema—and Machiavelli in renaissance Italy coerce the spectator into accepting a bourgeois system of morality and behaviour. He then shows how Brecht changed the spectator from passive empathiser to active thinker, roused to want to change the world that brought about the situations in the play instead of believing them to be inevitable and unchangeable. He describes how his own methods take this further by putting the spectators, rather than actors standing in for them, into the dramatic action with the power to change the result. Boal coined the term 'spect-actor' to describe this new type of spectator.

In his experiments in Peru in 1973, Boal devised a system of exercises to allow the participants to become aware of their own bodies and to learn to use them expressively.

First Stage: Knowing the Body

The purpose of these exercises is to make the participants more aware of their bodies and how they are shaped by their work and social class so that they can create characters from different professions and classes by using their bodies in different ways. The following examples are from Boal's own exercises.

Slow motion race

As a whole group, run a race in slow motion; the winner is the one who finishes last. You are not allowed to stop moving at any time during the race and you must take the largest steps you can and raise your foot above knee level on each step.

Hypnosis

Get into groups of two: A and B. A holds her hand a few centimetres from B's face, then moves it around in all directions at various speeds. B must move so that his face is always the same distance from A's hand. Swap over and repeat. Once you have mastered this, try it in groups of three where A controls one of the others with each hand. You could develop this further to groups of four, using both hands and one foot, or five, using both hands and both feet.

Boxing match
Stage a boxing match in pairs, but without touching one another at all. However you must both fight as though the fight was real and react as though you have really been hit. A development of this exercise, which Boal named *Out West*, takes place in an imaginary western movie, where a fight breaks out in a Wild West saloon using chairs, bottles, tables and anything else that may be found there. However, no one is allowed to actually touch anyone else and all objects are imaginary.

Second Stage: Making the Body Expressive

These exercises develop the ability to express through the body rather than through words.

The expressive body
Write the names of animals—there should be two of each animal: one male and one female—on some slips of paper and fold them up. Take one slip of paper each at random without showing it to anyone else. You must then give a physical impression of the animal on your slip of paper. No words or sounds are allowed. You then need to find your 'mate'—the person playing the same animal as you. Once you think you have found them, leave the game together without discussing whether you are correct. The object of the game is to learn physical expression, not to guess correctly. This exercise can be extended to express all sorts of other types of things—Boal suggests occupations or professions.

Third Stage: The Theatre as Language

This is theatre as a living language rather than something prepared in advance and presented as a finished product.

Spectators play an active part in deciding how the stage action proceeds and are not simply passive receivers. Boal divides this stage into three degrees of involvement.

First degree: *Simultaneous dramaturgy.* A short scene, ten to twenty minutes long, is performed by the actors from a theme proposed by someone in the community either by improvising from a prepared script or by creating the scene as it is performed. The scene stops at the moment of crisis and the actors ask the spectators for solutions to the problem. The actors act out each suggestion, and the spectators are allowed to intervene and correct the actors' words and actions. The spectators decide which, if any, of the solutions offered provides the best way to tackle the problem.

Simultaneous dramaturgy

As a whole group, brainstorm ideas for situations that will create a crisis where a decision has to be made about how to proceed. This should be something relevant to you, that could happen—or that has happened—to you or a member of your group (Boal gives examples of situations he has used, but they were relevant to the people he was working with and are unlikely to have any relevance to your group). Working in smaller groups, each group should create an outline of a scene lasting about ten to twenty minutes ending at the point of crisis when a decision has to be made about how to solve the problem. Perform these short plays to the whole group, and at the end take suggestions from spectators about how to proceed. Each suggestion must be acted out in full; care should be taken to follow the spectator's suggestion precisely, showing all of the good and bad consequences of carrying out this action. Spectators can intervene to correct words or actions of the actors to try to achieve a better resolution.

In simultaneous dramaturgy, the barrier between actor and spectator has been removed. The results of actions are not seen as inevitable or 'fate' because they can be changed as many times as necessary by the spectators to try to achieve the result they desire.

Second degree: *Image theatre.* Again the participants choose a subject of common interest that they wish to discuss, which can be something large, global or even abstract or a small, specific, local problem. One person begins by expressing an opinion on the topic, but no words are allowed; instead, the 'sculptor-participant' or 'spectator-sculptor' must mould the other participants into a frozen image or tableau that makes his or her opinion clear. This image is used to provoke a discussion, but again no words are allowed and others can only express their opinions by altering the images. Once an image is agreed on for the situation as it exists—the *actual image*—the spectator-sculptor creates a new image of the situation as he or she would want it to be—the *ideal image*. A third image is then created that goes between the other two, the *transitional image*, that shows how it may be possible to move from the *actual image* to the *ideal image*. This process forces participants to fully describe the problem and look for a feasible way of solving it, all using just three images and no words.

Image theatre

As a group, choose a problem to work on, which could be worldwide, in your country, in your local area or something at home, college, school or work. Somebody, preferably the person who made the original suggestion, creates a still image from the bodies of as many members of the group as are needed to represent the problem. Others can look at the image and change it until a final version of the *actual image* is agreed upon. All this must be done without speaking. The original spectator-sculptor then creates an *ideal image* in the same way to show how things could be if the problem was solved. A third *transitional image* is then created to try to find the step between the other two images—the path to solving the problem. Other suggestions are taken for this image, still without speaking. You should take your time with this exercise to make each image as real and complete as possible. This is not a classroom drama game—it is a method for trying to solve real, often complex, problems and empowering people to take control of their destinies using theatre techniques.

Third degree: *Forum theatre.* Again the group suggests a problem and a possible solution. The actors put together a ten or fifteen minute play to show the problem and the proposed solution, and then the participants are asked whether they agree with it. Somebody will invariably say that they do not. The scene is repeated exactly as before, but this time any spectator can replace any actor to try to steer the scene in a different direction (the actor waits on one side, ready to resume their role once their replacement considers their contribution to be complete). The other actors continue the scene, improvising their responses to the new actor's contributions. No one is allowed to simply explain their views—they must demonstrate how their idea works (and by doing so they may find out that it doesn't). Boal explains, 'Often a person is very revolutionary when in a public forum he envisages and advocates revolutionary and heroic acts; on the other hand, he often realizes that things are not so easy when he himself has to practice what he suggests.' As an example, he tells of a suggestion to use a bomb from someone who found, when he came to enact his suggestion, that he had no idea how to go about making or throwing a bomb, or the suggestion of a strike to protest about working conditions in a place that had such high unemployment and poverty that the foreman could simply go and hire other people to replace those on strike.

Forum theatre

In small groups, each group must create a problem and a possible solution relevant to people in the group within a ten to fifteen minute play. Each of these is performed in front of the whole group and the audience is asked whether the solution offered is the correct one. If anyone believes that it isn't, the scene is performed again but any spectator can join the action in place of any actor at any point and try to steer the scene in a more favourable direction. There should be no discussion of possible solutions, only action within the scenes to demonstrate how problems can be solved.

Forum theatre does not offer solutions to problems; instead it gives the people affected by the problems the means to find their own solutions that work for them. They get the opportunity to rehearse various possibilities in a safe, fictional environment before attempting to carry out their ideas for real with more serious consequences. Boal terms this a *rehearsal of revolution*:

Maybe the theater in itself is not revolutionary, but these theatrical forms are without a doubt a rehearsal of revolution. The truth of the matter is that the spectator-actor practices a real act even though he does it in a fictional manner. When he rehearses throwing a bomb on stage, he is concretely rehearsing the way a bomb is thrown; acting out his attempt to organize a strike, he is concretely organising a strike. Within its fictitious limits, the experience is a concrete one.

Fourth Stage: The Theatre as Discourse

All of the methods described up to now are forms of what Boal called 'rehearsal-theatre' rather than 'spectacle-theatre'—in other words, the performance is not a 'finished' piece of theatre but an open-ended story that is only completed during its performance. However Theatre of the Oppressed is also able to accommodate finished performances that are planned out in advance. Boal describes a few of these types of performances that he has used.

1. *Newspaper Theatre*. Performances are created from current news items using a number of different methods.

Items may simply be read out from newspapers, perhaps using a particular style, two items may be read together to illuminate one another, extra information such as statistics, slides and songs may be added and so on. A scene created from the item may be acted out, or it may be mimed to accompany an article reading, or similar events set in different periods of history or in different societies may be shown.

2. *Invisible Theatre.* This is theatre in a public place such as a shop, a street or a restaurant where the people who witness the action are not aware that what they are seeing is a performance by actors. A short piece must be carefully prepared and rehearsed, and the actors must anticipate every possible reaction from members of the public and rehearse their responses. Boal makes it clear that Invisible Theatre is not Guerrilla Theatre as the latter still maintains a separation between performers and spectators whereas Invisible Theatre involves the unaware spectators in the action and the subsequent discussion and never reveals itself as a performance. The performance is based on an issue that will provoke the spectators into discussion. For instance, one Invisible Theatre piece that Boal describes was performed in a restaurant: one of the actors ordered something expensive from the menu and ate it, then said he was unable to pay but would pay with his labour. This started a discussion between the actor, the waiter and others in the restaurant—provoked by other actors playing other customers—about how much workers in the restaurant were paid and how those who worked there could only afford the cheapest meals. There was a collection to pay for the meal to which some contributed and others objected, and the discussion raised by the performance went on through the night. Once again, performance is used to provoke people into examining their own problems and searching for possible solutions.

3. *Photo-romance.* The participants are given a basic storyline to act out, but they are not told that it is taken from a 'photo-romance' story, 'sub-literature on the lowest imaginable level, which furthermore always

serves as a vehicle for the ruling classes' ideology'. Once the acted-out version is shown, the original photo-romance story is produced and the two are compared; the participants will immediately take an active, critical role towards the story rather than the passive spectator role they would normally take. In particular, the lifestyles of the characters and how the writer has put forward certain types of behaviour and ideology as acceptable are examined. The same technique was used in Peru to analyse television programmes.

4. *Breaking of repression*. Boal contends that some groups of people dominate other groups, whether divided by class, age, race or gender, using repression and force, not discussion or agreement: 'The ruling classes, the old, the "superior" races, or the masculine sex, have their sets of values and impose them by force, by unilateral violence, upon the oppressed classes, the young, the races they consider inferior, or women.' He also argues that repression is not something general and abstract between groups of people but is based on specific, concrete acts committed by individuals from one group on individuals from another group. In order to break this cycle, Boal asked his participants to remember one specific incident when they felt oppressed and were forced to act against their own desires. One person's story is reconstructed as a theatre piece in detail, recreating every action and feeling exactly as they occurred. The story is repeated, but this time the protagonist should not accept the repression and should instead fight for his own desires or ideas. This is another example of *rehearsal of revolution*; the participant gets the opportunity to try out methods of resisting repression in a safe environment to see what the consequences might be if this were done in real life.

5. *Myth theatre*. This is not so much a type of performance as another place to look for methods of repression and control, although they can be investigated using theatre. Local myths are sometimes used to control people's behaviour and to conceal the real reasons for something. Boal gives the example of a local legend

about ghosts inhabiting the top of a mountain, which said that no one who went there ever returned. When one brave young man climbed to the top, instead of ghosts he found some Americans who owned a gold mine. Another story justified one man's ownership of a lagoon that was the only source of fresh water in a particular area—of course he sold the water to others and made a lot of money—with a tale of a mysterious stranger who promised to give this man a lagoon to benefit everyone in the area as long as he gave him his eldest daughter. Myths are sometimes used in this way to justify a system that benefits some and represses others, and theatre can be used to reveal this.

6. *Analytical theatre.* A story is suggested by a participant and is acted out by the actors. The main characters are each analysed and broken down into all of their social roles, and an object is chosen to represent each role that each character represents. Boal gives an example of a story in which a policeman kills a chicken thief. The policeman fulfils a number of social roles, including 'a) he is a worker because he rents his labor-power; symbol: a pair of overalls; b) He is a bourgeois because he protects private property and values it more than human life; symbol: a necktie, or a top hat, etc.; c) he is a repressive agent because he is a policeman; symbol: a revolver.' Symbols must be chosen by the group, as different objects will mean different things to different people. The story is told again, but this time some of the symbols are taken away from each character or given to another character, and the social role that goes with the object is transferred with it, such as taking the necktie—and therefore the bourgeois role—away from the policeman, or giving the robber a necktie as well. The exercise is meant to show that 'human actions are not the exclusive and primordial result of individual psychology: almost always, through the individual speaks his class!'

7. *Rituals and masks.* Rituals are fixed patterns of actions or behaviour that reveal the nature of a society and the relationships between people in that society. Masks are

the roles that are imposed on people within that society by the part they play in these rituals. As an example, Boal proposed a scene in which a man goes to a priest to confess his sins. The scene is performed four times with both priest and parishioner as landlords, the priest as a landlord and the parishioner as a peasant, the priest as a peasant and the parishioner as a landlord and both priest and parishioner as peasants. In each case the ritual of confessing sins is identical, but the different social masks will make the four scenes completely different.

Theatre as discourse

Try to create your own performance based on some of the methods of Theatre as Discourse described above. For instance:

- Find a newspaper article that seems to be expressing a particular point of view or that perhaps does not give a full picture of the circumstances with all of the facts. Stage this article by reading it out whilst simultaneously performing a scene that shows the opposing point of view, or have it read out by a character that you think characterises the point of view being declared (for instance, a politician from the far left or right, a military leader, a civil servant, a teacher).

- Find an issue that may provoke discussion, plan a short performance to raise the issue and find a location to perform it as a piece of Invisible Theatre. For instance, you may wish to create something about the homeless on the streets with your actors playing beggars and passers-by, or about a local by-law that few people know about, or about the building of a shopping centre or new road. Remember that the point of Invisible Theatre is to stimulate discussion amongst real people provoked by the actors—this is not a practical joke. You should not reveal that you are actors at any stage or the participants may feel cheated and disregard the whole thing.

You may also wish to look at some of the other ideas listed above, or create a performance from a combination of these elements.

Sample Questions

1. Discuss the following statement in relation to invisible theatre: if an audience is not aware that it is watching a performance then it is not really theatre.
2. In what ways did Boal build on the ideas of Brecht?
3. What methods did Boal use to help people to find solutions to their own problems rather than telling them what to do?

Further Reference

Konstantin Stanislavski

Bibliography

Benedetti, Jean, *Stanislavski & the Actor* (London: Methuen, 1998). A very good workbook for anyone wishing to learn Stanislavski's methods of actor training and rehearsal.

Benedetti, Jean, *Stanislavski: An Introduction* (London: Methuen, 1989). A short summary of Stanislavski's life and work.

Benedetti, Jean, *Stanislavski: His Life and Art* (London: Methuen, 1999). A thorough and entertaining biography. This revised edition contains a great deal of information that was unknown outside Russia when the first edition came out in 1988.

Braun, Edward, *The Director and the Stage: From Naturalism To Grotowski* (London: Methuen, 1982). An excellent book recounting the history of directing in the theatre. Contains a chapter on Stanislavski and Chekhov.

Hodge, Alison (ed.), *Twentieth Century Actor Training* (London and New York: Routledge, 2000). Contains a chapter on Stanislavski's system written by Sharon Carnicke.

Jones, David Richard, *Great Directors at Work: Stanislavsky, Brecht, Kazan, Brook* (Berkeley: University of California Press, 1986). The first chapter looks in detail at Stanislavski's production of Chekhov's *The Seagull*.

Roose-Evans, James, *Experimental Theatre: from Stanislavski to Peter Brook* (London: Routledge, 1989). Contains some information about Stanislavski.

Stanislavski, Constantin, *An Actor Prepares*, translated by Elizabeth Reynolds Hapgood (London: Methuen, 1980). The first and most popular book by Stanislavski on the 'system'.

Stanislavski, Constantin, *Building A Character*, translated by Elizabeth Reynolds Hapgood (London: Methuen, 1968). A version of the proposed second half of *An Actor's Work On Himself*, left incomplete when Stanislavski died.

Stanislavski, Constantin, *Creating A Role*, translated by Elizabeth Reynolds Hapgood (London: Methuen, 1981). Published as a sequel to the other two books on the system, but compiled from various notes of Stanislavski's long after his death.

Styan, J L, *Modern drama in theory and practice 1: Realism and Naturalism* (Cambridge: Cambridge University Press, 1981). Contains a chapter on the Moscow Art Theatre's contribution to realism.

Edward Gordon Craig

Bibliography

Braun, Edward, *The Director and the Stage: From Naturalism To Grotowski* (London: Methuen, 1982). Contains a chapter on Craig, describing the events of his life and work.

Craig, Edward, *Gordon Craig: The Story of His Life* (London: Gollancz, 1968). A complete biography of Craig by his son.

Roose-Evans, James, *Experimental Theatre: from Stanislavski to Peter Brook* (London: Routledge, 1989). Contains a chapter on Craig and Adolphe Appia, who was working on similar ideas to Craig independently at the same time.

Rosenfeld, Sybil, *A Short History of Scene Design in Great Britain* (Oxford: Basil Blackwell, 1973). Contains a section about Craig's work, and also some information about his father, Edward Godwin, and his work in the theatre.

Senelick, Laurence, *Gordon Craig's Moscow Hamlet: a reconstruction* (London: Greenwood Press, 1982). As its title says, this book reconstructs Craig and Stanislavski's production of *Hamlet*.

Styan, J L, *Modern drama in theory and practice 2: Symbolism, Surrealism and the Absurd* (Cambridge: Cambridge University Press, 1981). Contains a short section on Craig's stage design.

Walton, J Michael (ed), *Craig On Theatre* (London: Methuen, 1983). Excerpts from various written works by Craig with a few of his illustrations. A good selection of his work, giving a good overview of his ideas.

Internet

The Ellen Terry Tribute Page http://www.ellenterry.org/ This website, dedicated to Craig's mother, contains a biography and photos of him and some of his engravings.

Antonin Artaud

Bibliography

Artaud, Antonin, *The Theatre and its Double*, translated by Victor Corti (London: Calder, 1993). This may not be a great translation of Artaud's most famous collection of essays and letters but it is still the only full English version and therefore essential reading for any in-depth study of his work.

Barber, Stephen, *Blows and Bombs* (London: Creation Books, 1999). A recently updated biography of Artaud, which is very thorough, detailed and up-to-date.

Barber, Stephen, *The Screaming Body* (London: Creation Books, 1999). This book focuses on Artaud's poetry, drawings, film work and work for radio, but is an excellent study of these aspects of his work.

Braun, Edward, *The Director and the Stage: From Naturalism To Grotowski* (London: Methuen, 1982). Contains a chapter on Artaud's Theatre of Cruelty.

Esslin, Martin, *Antonin Artaud: The Man and His Work* (London: Calder, 1999). A thorough study of Artaud's life and work, especially his theatre work.

Roose-Evans, James, *Experimental Theatre: from Stanislavski to Peter Brook* (London: Routledge, 1989). The chapter 'The Theatre of Ecstasy' covers Artaud and others.

Stoppelman, Gabriela, *Artaud for Beginners*, illustrated by Jorge Hardmeier, translated by Caroline Maldonado (New York: Writers and Readers, 2000). A good summary of Artaud's life and work in comic book format.

Styan, J L, *Modern drama in theory and practice 2: Symbolism, Surrealism and the Absurd* (Cambridge: Cambridge University Press, 1981). A chapter on Theatre of Cruelty links Artaud with Peter Brook.

Videography

Dreyer, Carl, *The Passion of Joan of Arc* (Criterion, 1999).

Pabst, G W, *Threepenny Opera* (London: British Film Institute, 1998). This video contains both the French and German versions of the film. Artaud was in the French version.

Internet

Antonin Artaud http://www.antoninartaud.org/home.html A site dedicated to Artaud. There is not much information here and much of it is in French, but it is notable for providing the opportunity to hear Artaud's own voice in an excerpt from *To Have Done with the Judgement of God.*

Bertolt Brecht

Bibliography

Benjamin, Walter, *Understanding Brecht*, introduced by Stanley Mitchell, translated by Anna Bostock (London: Verso, 1998). An excellent description and analysis of many of Brecht's techniques written by someone who knew him well.

Berlau, Ruth, Bertolt Brecht, Claus Hubalek, Peter Palitzsch, Käthe Rülicke (eds), *Theaterarbeit: 6 Aufführungen des Berliner Ensembles* (Berlin and Frankfurt am Main: Suhrkamp, 1961). Information from the model books of six of Brecht's later productions together with other writings. Although it is in German, there are lots of photographs that are very useful for seeing how specific moments in the plays worked in performance.

Braun, Edward, *The Director and the Stage: From Naturalism To Grotowski* (London: Methuen, 1982). Contains a chapter 'Brecht's Formative Years'.

Brecht, Bertolt, *Brecht on Theatre: The Development of an Aesthetic*, edited and translated by John Willet (London: Methuen, 1964). This is still the most complete volume of Brecht's various writings on theatre available in English and an essential work for an in-depth study of his ideas and theories.

Brecht, Bertolt, *Collected Plays: Five*, edited and introduced by John Willet and Ralph Manheim (London: Methuen, 1995). Contains scripts of *Life of Galileo* and *Mother Courage and her Children* together with extensive notes translated from the *Couragemodell* that show how Brecht worked on the play for his own production in 1949.

Eyre, Richard & Nicholas Wright, *Changing Stages: A view of British Theatre in the twentieth century* (London: Bloomsbury, 2000). The book of the BBC TV series. The chapter 'BB' is a selective but very readable biography of Brecht, in particular relating Brecht's life and his work to the wider political events in Germany and the rest of the world at the time.

Hodge, Alison (ed.), *Twentieth Century Actor Training* (London and New York: Routledge, 2000). A chapter by Peter Thomson looks at Brecht and actor training.

Jones, David Richard, *Great Directors at Work: Stanislavsky, Brecht, Kazan, Brook* (Berkeley: University of California Press, 1986). Contains a chapter analysing in great detail Brecht's work as a director, looking particularly at his production of *Mother Courage* in 1949 as described in the *Couragemodell*.

Roose-Evans, James, *Experimental Theatre: from Stanislavski to Peter Brook* (London: Routledge, 1989). One chapter looks at Reinhardt, Piscator and Brecht.

Thomson, Peter & Glendyr Sacks (editors), *The Cambridge Companion to Brecht* (Cambridge: Cambridge University Press, 1994). A collection of essays on different aspects of Brecht's life and work from some of the world's leading Brecht experts.

Thomson, Peter, *Brecht: Mother Courage and Her Children* (Cambridge: Cambridge University Press, 1997). A detailed analysis of the play and some of its most important productions.

Videography

Pabst, GW, *Threepenny Opera* (London: British Film Institute, 1998). This video contains both the French and German versions of the film.

Internet

International Brecht Society http://polyglot.lss.wisc.edu/german/brecht/ The website of the society set up to promote the understanding of Brecht's work. According to the introductory page, 'The International Brecht Society Homepage is maintained as a service to scholars, critics, students, and theater people round the world who are interested in the works and thought of Brecht.'

Marxists.org Internet Archive http://www.marxists.org.uk/ This website contains a huge amount of information about Marxism and Marxist writers, including Marx himself and Lenin. There is also some interesting information about dialectics.

Dialectics for Kids http://home.igc.org/~venceremos/index.htm A website specifically set up to explain dialectics in simple terms.

Jerzy Grotowski

Bibliography

Braun, Edward, *The Director and the Stage: From Naturalism To Grotowski* (London: Methuen, 1982). Contains a chapter by Jennifer Kumiega on 'Grotowski's Laboratory Theatre'.

Grotowski, Jerzy, *Towards A Poor Theatre* (London: Methuen, 1969). A collection of Grotowski's early writings about theatre and exercises.

Hodge, Alison (ed.), *Twentieth Century Actor Training* (London and New York: Routledge, 2000). Contains a chapter on Grotowski written by Lisa Wolford.

Kumiega, Jennifer, *The Theatre of Grotowski* (London: Methuen, 1985). Investigates the work of Grotowski.

Richards, Thomas, *At Work with Grotowski on Physical Actions* (New York and London: Routledge, 1995). A book on Grotowski's methods from his successor.

Roose-Evans, James, *Experimental Theatre: from Stanislavski to Peter Brook* (London: Routledge, 1989). Contains two chapters on Grotowski's work, one on Poor Theatre and one on his journey to the east.

Schechner, Richard and Lisa Wolford (eds), *The Grotowski Sourcebook* (London and New York: Routledge, 1997). A collection of essays from various writers about Grotowski.

Videography

Grotowski, Jerzy, *Akropolis* (New York: Arthur Cantor Films, 1971). A filmed performance from 1968 of Polish Theatre Laboratory's production of Wyspianski's play with an introduction featuring Peter Brook. The Polish dialogue is not translated and the English commentary is a bit sparse, but the impressive physical and vocal skills of leading Grotowski actors such as Ryszard Cieslak can be seen.

Internet

Source Material on Jerzy Grotowski http://owendaly.com/ jeff/grotdir.htm This site contains a number of documents and essays by and about Grotowski and his work, including newspaper reviews and examinations of his links with other practitioners and techniques including Artaud and Vakhtangov.

Grotowski: Igniting the Flame http://rgaffield.home. mindspring.com/grotowski.htm A detailed essay on Grotowski's life and work.

Peter Brook

Bibliography

Addenbrooke, David, *The Royal Shakespeare Company: The Peter Hall Years* (London: William Kimber, 1974). A book about the Royal Shakespeare Company that contains information about Brook and his RSC work.

Brook, Peter, *Evoking Shakespeare* (London: Nick Hern Books, 1999). A short book based on a lecture Brook gave in Berlin in 1996 that contains some fascinating ideas about Shakespeare's life, plays and poetry.

Brook, Peter, *The Empty Space* (London: Penguin, 1990). Brook's most famous printed work, and an essential read for anyone studying or interested in theatre, in which he describes the four types of theatre as he sees them.

Brook, Peter, *The Shifting Point: 40 years of theatrical exploration 1946–1987* (London: Methuen, 1987). A collection of essays by Brook on all aspects of theatre, including important theatre people such as Shakespeare, Beckett, Craig, Artaud, Grotowski and Gielgud.

Carrière, Jean-Claude, *The Mahabharata*, translated by Peter Brook (London: Methuen, 1988). The script of Brook's famous stage production.

Delgado, Maria M and Paul Heritage, *In Contact with the Gods? Directors Talk Theatre* (Manchester: Manchester University Press, 1996). Contains some biographical information about Brook and an interview with him conducted by Michael Billington in 1994.

Eyre, Richard & Nicholas Wright, *Changing Stages: A view of British Theatre in the twentieth century* (London: Bloomsbury, 2000). Contains some information about Brook and his work.

Heilpern, John, *The Conference of the Birds: The story of Peter Brook in Africa* (London: Methuen, 1989). An account of Brook's travels around Africa, which also examines how these experiments show the important aspects of Brook's work throughout his life.

Hodge, Alison (ed.), *Twentieth Century Actor Training* (London and New York: Routledge, 2000). Contains a chapter on Brook written by Lorna Marshall and David Williams.

Jones, David Richard, *Great Directors at Work: Stanislavsky, Brecht, Kazan, Brook* (Berkeley: University of California Press, 1986). Looks at Brook's work by focusing in great detail on the *Marat-Sade*.

Moffit, Dale (ed.), *Between Two Silences: Talking with Peter Brook* (London: Methuen, 2000). A jumbled collection of information from talks given by Brook in Dallas.

Styan, J L, *Modern drama in theory and practice 2: Symbolism, Surrealism and the Absurd* (Cambridge: Cambridge University Press, 1981). A chapter on Theatre of Cruelty links Artaud with Peter Brook.

Todd, Andrew & Jean-Guy Lecat, *The Open Circle: Peter Brook's Theatre Environments* (London: Faber and Faber, 2003). A hefty study of the performance spaces used by Brook, accompanied by lots of photographs.

Weiss, Peter, *Marat/Sade: The Persecution and Assassination of Marat as performed by the Inmates of the Asylum of Charenton under the direction of the Marquis de Sade*, English version by Geoffrey Skelton, verse adaptation by Adrian Mitchell (London: Marion Boyars, 1982). The script of Weiss's play in the version used for Brook's famous production.

Videography

Brook, Peter, *King Lear* (4 Front Video, 2002). The film of Brook's RSC production starring Paul Scofield.

Brook, Peter, *Lord of the Flies* (Warner Home Video, 1999). Brook's film of William Golding's novel.

Brook, Peter, *Marat/Sade* (MGM, 2000). Film of Brook's production.

Brook, Peter, *The Mahaharata* (Connoisseur Video, 1995). The television version of Brook's stage production on three videos.

Feil, Gerald, *The Empty Space* (Mystic Fire, 1994). Documents a 1970 visit by Brook and his group to the Brooklyn Academy of Music.

Internet

Platform Papers: Peter Brook http://nt-online.org/?lid=2632 A transcript of a platform event at London's National Theatre in 1993 in which Brook answers questions from the NT's Executive Director Genista McIntosh and from the audience.

The Readiness Is All: Peter Brook's Thirty Years in Paris http://www.shakespeare-bulletin.org/issues/winter01/article-savin.html An article by Janet Savin from the Winter 2001 edition of Shakespeare Bulletin.

Peter Brook interviewed by Faynia Williams http://www.dggb.co.uk/publications/article9_86.html An interview from 2001 for the magazine of the Directors' Guild of Great Britain when the Guild presented him with a Lifetime Achievement Award.

Augusto Boal

Bibliography

Boal, Augusto, *Games for Actors and Non-actors*, translated by Adrian Jackson (London: Routledge, 1992). Contains lots of Theatre of the Oppressed practical exercises.

Boal, Augusto, *Hamlet and the Baker's Son: My Life in Theatre and Politics*, translated by Adrian Jackson and Candida Baker (London and New York: Routledge, 2001). A very entertaining autobiography, full of colourful stories about his life, his family and his work.

Boal, Augusto, *Legislative Theatre*, translated by Adrian Jackson (London: Routledge, 1998). Boal describes his method of using Forum Theatre as part of the democratic process.

Boal, Augusto, *Theater of the Oppressed*, translated by Charles A and Maria-Odilia Leal McBride and Emily Fryer (London: Pluto Books, 1979). In this book, Boal argues that the dramaturgy of Aristotle and Machiavelli tries to coerce the spectator into a bourgeois way of behaviour. He shows how Brecht began to break down the barriers between spectators and actors and how his own ideas move on from Brecht's work.

Delgado, Maria M and Paul Heritage, *In Contact with the Gods? Directors Talk Theatre* (Manchester: Manchester University Press, 1996). Contains some biographical information and a transcript of a talk he gave in Manchester in 1995.

Internet

Community Arts Network: A Brief Introduction to Augusto Boal http://www.communityarts.net/readingroom/archive/boalintro.php As it says, a very brief introduction to Boal's work, followed by an interview with him in Omaha, Nebraska in 1996 and a glossary of Theatre of the Oppressed terms.

Theater of The Oppressed Laboratory http://www.toplab.org/ Contains lots of information about Boal and the Theatre of the Oppressed.

Northern Visions: Interview with Augusto Boal http://www.northernvisions.org/boal.htm An undated lengthy interview with Boal in Belfast.

Glossary of Terms

alienation Using various techniques to make the audience see something familiar as though it was something strange to them, in order to make them question its validity.

blocking 1. The arrangement of *actors* on a stage. 2. Obscuring the audience's view of an *actor*.

catharsis According to Aristotle, a purifying of the emotions brought about through watching tragic drama.

chorus In Greek theatre, a group of people that told the story to the audience. Now often used to describe any crowds of people on stage without named parts, particularly if they sing together.

cop in the head Boal's term for a kind of oppression from within the mind, where something in our own head prevents us from doing what we really want to do.

courtesan actor Grotowski's name for an actor who tries to please the audience and responds to its reactions rather than giving himself totally to the performance.

cyc, cyclorama A stretched cloth used as the backdrop to the stage, which can be coloured using lighting, or projected onto.

deadly theatre Brook's name for bad theatre.

dialectical materialism From Marxist theory, a belief in materialism—the philosophical concept that the world is ruled by matter rather than ideas—and dialectics—a method of discourse in which an idea and its opposite are debated in order to find a resolution based on both.

downstage The part of the stage nearest to the audience. See also *upstage; stage left; stage right.*

end stage A stage configuration in which all the audience views the acting space from one side.

epic theatre Brecht's various methods of forcing the audience to think about the situations presented in the play and to form an opinion on them rather than feeling empathy for the characters.

forum theatre Boal's form of theatre that allows spectators get on to the stage, take the place of one of the actors and try to bring the play to a more satisfactory resolution.

found space A space used for performance that was built for a purpose other than theatre, such as a factory or warehouse, that uses the existing architecture of the building rather than converting it into a theatre.

fourth wall A concept in naturalistic theatre in which the *proscenium arch* opening is treated as one of four walls in a room and the presence of the audience is not acknowledged by the actors.

gest Something, such as a word, gesture, way of speaking, that indicates the attitude of a character. A **social gest** indicates the character's attitude to others.

gobo A pierced metal or printed glass disc placed into a focused spotlight to shape the light or project a particular shape onto the stage.

holy actor An actor who gives himself totally to the performance, sacrificing himself for the benefit of spectators.

holy theatre A theatre of ritual and sacrifice that tries to fulfil the same role as religion once had in society.

immediate theatre A theatre that creates everything anew for each performance rather than assuming older notions about the play or about theatre in general to be correct and unchangeable.

improvisation Creating drama without a script, at least partly making it up during the performance.

impulse Grotowski's name for something that begins right inside the actor's body as the root of any action that the actor performs.

invisible theatre Boal's form of theatre that begins a fictional situation in a real setting to provoke debate between observers who do not know that the situation has been staged.

legislative theatre Boal's use of Theatre of the Oppressed techniques to allow people to contribute to the democratic process.

Lehrstück A teaching play; one of Brecht's early plays written to education those who performed it.

opposite prompt (OP) *Stage right*, the side opposite where the *prompt* traditionally sits.

promenade A stage configuration in which each scene takes place in a different place and the audience moves to see it.

prompt 1. The person *on the book* who feeds a line to an actor if they forget it during a performance or rehearsal. 2. Also the name given to a line given to an actor by the person on the book to remind them where they are up to. 3. *Stage left*, the side of the stage the prompt traditionally sits. Sometimes denoted by 'P' in old scripts.

proscenium; proscenium arch A type of end stage with an arch or picture frame around it.

rehearsal of revolution Boal's term for the process of using theatre to look for solutions for real problems in a safe fictional situation.

rough theatre A type of theatre that mixes styles, can be performed anywhere such as an inn yard or the back of a cart, uses whatever comes to hand for props and costumes and is often vulgar and anti-establishment.

spect-actor Boal's term for a spectator who is also able to become part of the action and influence the outcome of the drama.

stage left; stage right The left or right of an *actor* stood in the centre of the stage facing the audience. See also *upstage, downstage*.

theatre of the oppressed Boal's theatre, which uses theatre techniques to help people find solutions to political and personal problems.

theatre-in-the-round A stage configuration in which the audience completely surrounds the acting space.

thrust A stage configuration in which the audience occupies three of the four sides of either the whole acting space or an area that extends forward from it.

traverse A stage configuration in which the audience occupies two opposing sides of the acting space.

upstage The part of the stage furthest away from the audience. See also *downstage; stage left; stage right*.

via negativa Grotowski's term for an approach to training and production that removes everything that is not necessary and blocking progress rather than adding to what is there.

Index

Abbey Theatre, Dublin, 45
Acis and Galatea (Handel), 30
action, 8, 26
Actor and The Über-marionette, The (Craig), 39
Actors' Studio, The, 138
Adamov, Arthur, 52
adaptation, 20–21
Adler, Stella, 6
after-time, 25
Akropolis (Wyspianski), 92
Aldwych Theatre, London, 115
alienation, 75–78, 167
An Actor Prepares (Stanislavski), 4, 5, 7, 8, 10, 24
An Actor's Work on A Role (Stanislavski), 4–5
An Actor's Work on Himself (Stanislavski), 3, 4, 5, 24
analytical theatre, 150
anti-Aristotlean, 68
Antigone (Brecht), 82
antithesis, 72
Apocalypsis cum •guris, 92
Arden, John, 140
Arena Goldoni, 31
Aristotle, 142
art as performance, 95
art as vehicle, 94–95
Artaud, Antonin, 49–64, 111, 114, 127, 135, 157–158
Artists of the Theatre of the Future, The (Craig), 40
Atreus (Seneca), 51

Baal (Brecht), 65
Baden-Baden Music Festival, 82
Balinese dance, 50, 54
Barba, Eugenio, 92

Barrault, Jean-Louis, 52, 140
basic action, 26, 27
Beckett, Samuel, 131
before-time, 25
Beggar's Opera, The (Gay), 114
Benjamin, Walter, 78
Berliner Ensemble, 66, 67
Bethlehem (Housman), 30
Bible, 58
biomechanics, 98
Birmingham Repertory Theatre, 113
Blin, Roger, 52
Blood Of A Poet, The (Cocteau), 50
Boal, Augusto, 81, 135, 137–153, 164–165
Boleslavski, Richard, 3, 6
Bouffes du Nord, Paris, 116
Brahm, Otto, 31
Braque, Georges, 52
breaking of repression, 149
Brecht On Theatre (Brecht), 67
Brecht, Bertolt, 65–90, 123, 130, 131, 142, 153, 158–160
Breton, André, 52
Brook, Peter, 59, 94, 113–135, 140, 161–164
Building A Character (Stanislavski), 5

Carmen (Bizet), 116
Casarès, Marie, 52
Censi, The (Shelly), 51, 57
Chairs, The (Ionesco), 92
Chanticleer Theatre, South Kensington, 113
Chekhov, Anton, 138
Chekhov, Michael, 3
CICT, 116

Cieslak, Ryszard, 103, 109
circles of attention, 12–14
CIRT, 116
Columbia University, 138
Comédie des Champs-Elysées, 50
communion, 19–20
concentration of attention,
    10–14
Conference of the Birds
    (Heilpern), 118
Conference of the Birds,
    The (Brook), 116
Conquest of Mexico (Artaud), 51
Constant Prince, The (Calderón),
    92, 103, 109
cop in the head, 141, 167
Coronet Theatre, Los Angeles, 66
corporels, 98, 99–100
Correio Paulistano, 138
costume, 63, 96, 104, 132
counter through-action, 25–26, 27
Couragemodell (Brecht), 84–88
courtesan actor, 103, 167
Covent Garden, 114
Craig, Edward Gordon, 3, 25,
    28–47, 156–157
Creating A Role (Stanislavski), 5
Cynkutis, Zbigniew, 103

Dalcroze's eurhythmics, 98, 100
deadly theatre, 122–126, 131, 167
Death of a Salesman (Miller), 42
Decision, The (Brecht), 82
Delsarte, François, 98, 100
Demain, 49
design, 42–46, 60, 77, 96,
    132–133
Deutches Theater, Berlin, 66
dialectical materialism, 72–73, 167
dialectics, 70, 71–75
Dido and Aeneas (Purcell), 29
Doll's House, A (Ibsen), 41
Dostoevsky, Fyodor, 138
Dr Faustus (Marlowe), 92, 103,
    106, 107, 108, 113
dramatic theatre, 68–69

Drums in the Night (Brecht), 65
Duchamp, Marcel, 52
Dullin, Charles, 49, 52, 98
Duncan, Isadora, 31, 32
Duse, Eleonore, 31, 39

Elizabethan theatre, 130
emotion memory, 16–19
Empty Space, The (Brook), 115,
    117–118, 122
Engel, Erich, 65
epic theatre, 67–70, 168
episode, 26
Escola de Arte Dramatica, 138
Evgeni Onegin (Tchaikovski), 4
Exception and the Rule,
    The (Brecht), 71

fact, 26, 27
faschists, 65, 79
Fedotov, Aleksandr, 2
Férdière, Gaston, 51–52
First Studio, 3
Flaszen, Ludwik, 92
Flight over the Ocean,
    The (Brecht), 65, 82
Forefather's Eve (Mickiewicz),
    92, 108
forum theatre, 140, 141,
    146–147, 168
Freud, Sigmund, 56

Gassner, John, 138
gest, 78–80, 168
Giacommetti, Alberto, 52
Giehse, Therese, 84
Gielgud, John, 114
given circumstances, 9–10, 25, 103
Godwin, Edward William, 29
Goethe, Johann Wolfgang von,
    67–68
Gorky, Makim, 138
Grotowski, Jerzy, 91–111, 115,
    118, 120, 127–128, 135,
    160–161
Group Theatre, New York, 6

Hamlet (Shakespeare), 3, 25, 32, 35, 41, 45, 104, 109, 113, 117, 138

Hamlet and the Baker's Son (Boal), 141

Hampstead Conservatoire of Music, 30

hatha yoga, 98

Hauptmann, Elisabeth, 65

He Said No (Brecht), 82

He Said Yes (Brecht), 82

Hegel, Georg Wilhelm Friedrich, 72–73

Heilpern, John, 118, 121

Heliogabalus (Artaud), 51

Henry IV (Shakespeare), 130–131

Hitler, Adolf, 65

holy actor, 103, 168

holy theatre, 59, 126–129, 131, 135, 168

Horse and the Saint, The (Boal), 138

Hour Glass, The (Yeats), 45

House Across the Street, The (Boal), 138

House Un-American Activities Committee, 66

Hughes, Ted, 116

if, 10

image theatre, 141, 145–146

imagination, 10–16

immediate theatre, 131–134, 168

impulse, 99, 120, 169

In the Jungle of Cities (Brecht), 65

Infernal Machine (Cocteau), 113

inner monologue, 26–27

inorganic, 33–35

invisible theatre, 140, 141, 148, 169

Irving, Henry, 29, 39

Jacobs, Sally, 115

joker, 139

Kathakali, 98

Katzgraben (Strittmater), 71

Kew Theatre, 113

King Lear (Shakespeare), 60, 107, 114, 123

Kordian (Slowacki), 108

La Passion de Jeanne d'Arc (Dreyer), 50

La Révolution Surréaliste, 50

Laboratory Theatre of 13 Rows, 92, 93

LAMDA, 114

Laughton, Charles, 66, 77

legislative theatre, 141, 169

Lehrstücke, 65, 80–82, 169

Leigh, Vivien, 114

Lessing Theatre, Berlin, 31

Lester, Adrian, 117

Life of Galileo (Brecht), 66, 74–75, 76, 77

lighting, 60–61, 96, 132

Lord of the Flies (Golding/ Brook), 114

Losey, Joseph, 66

Love Scenes (Slowacki), 92

Love's Labours Lost (Shakespeare), 113, 133

Lugné-Poe, Aurélien, 49

Lyceum Theatre, 29

L'Engrenage (Sartre, Boal), 138

L'Homme Qui (The Man Who), 117

Macbeth (Shakespeare), 46, 58, 107, 109, 132

Machiavelli, Niccolò, 142

Maeterlinck, 42

Magdalen College, Oxford, 113

Mahabharata, The (Carrière), 117

Mali Theatre, 2

Malin Studio, New York, 138

Man and Superman (Shaw), 113

Man Who Mistook His Wife For A Hat, The (Sacks), 117

Marat-Sade (Weiss), 114, 115

Marquis de Sade, 58

Marx, Karl, 65, 71, 72

Mask, The, 31, 32
masks, 150–151
Masque of Love, The (Purcell), 30
Measures Taken, The (Brecht), 82
Meierhold, Vsevolod, 3, 92, 98
mental images, 26–27
Method, 6
Method of Physical Actions, 4, 24–25, 28, 98
Mianowska, Aleksandra, 92
Midsummer Night's Dream, A (Shakespeare), 38, 41, 115
Miller, Arthur, 140
mis-en-scène, 2
Mitchell, Adrian, 115
Mnouchkine, Arianne, 140
model books, 82–89, 90
Molière, 123
Month in the Country, A (Turgenev), 3
Moscow Art Theatre, 2, 3, 4, 32, 137–138
Mother Courage and her Children (Brecht), 42, 66, 75, 77, 83–88, 135
Mother, The (Brecht), 65, 80
Much Ado About Nothing (Shakespeare), 31
Munich Kammerspiel, 65
Müller, Heiner, 81
My Life In Art (Stanislavski), 4, 5
myth theatre, 149–150

Nancy Festival, 140
Napoléon (Gance), 50
Nazi Party, 65, 66, 79
Neher, Casper, 89
Nemirovich-Danchenko, Vladimir Ivanovich, 2, 3
newspaper theatre, 140, 141, 147–148
No More Masterpieces (Artaud), 56, 57–58
No Trifling With Love (De Musset), 29

Nouvelle Revue Française, 50, 51

object of attention, 10–12
objective drama, 93–94
Oedipus the King (Sophocles), 109
Of Mice And Men (Steinbeck), 138
Olivier, Laurence, 114
On Epic and Dramatic Poetry (Goethe/Schiller), 67–68
On Gestic Music (Brecht), 79
On The Art of the Theatre (Craig), 31, 32, 35
Opera Studio, 4, 21
organic, 33–35
Orghast (Hughes), 116
Othello (Shakespeare), 40
Oxford University Film Society, 113

Page, The, 29
paratheatre, 92–93
Peer Gynt (Ibsen), 46
photo-romance, 148–149
Picasso, Pablo, 52
Piscator, Erwin, 67
Pitoeff, George, 49
plastiques, 100, 101
Poetics (Aristotle), 67
poor theatre, 95–110
Pretenders,The (Ibsen), 32
Production and Metaphysics (Artaud), 53
Purcell Operatic Society, 29
Pygmalion (Shaw), 113

Rearrangements (Craig), 33
rehearsal of revolution, 147, 149, 169
relaxation, 7
Resistable Rise of Arturo Ui, The (Brecht), 140
rich theatre, 95
Richard III (Shakespeare), 107
Richards, Thomas, 95
Rise and Fall of the City Mahagonny, The (Brecht), 68

rituals, 150–151
Rivière, Jacques, 50, 52
Robart, Maude, 95
Rodrigues, Nelson, 137
Romeo and Juliet (Shakespeare),
    46, 107, 114
Rosmersholm (Ibsen), 31, 35–36
rough theatre, 129–131, 135, 169
Royal Shakespeare Company,
    114, 118
Royal Theatre Copenhagen, 32

Saint-Denis, Michel, 114
Sartre, Jean Paul, 52, 140
Scene (Craig), 44
Schaustück, 81
Schechner, Richard, 93, 140
Schiller, Friedrich, 67–68
Scofield, Paul, 113
screens, 44
Seagull, The (Chekhov), 2
*Seashell and the Clergyman, The
    (Artaud / Dulac)*, 50
Seminário de Dramaturgia, 138
sensory memory, 17–18
*Sentimental Journey through
    France and Italy, A (Stern/
    Brook)*, 113
Shakespeare Memorial Theatre,
    113
Shakespeare, William, 58, 118,
    123, 125, 130, 131, 135, 138
Shaw, Martin, 29–30
Shchepkin, Mikhaïl, 2
Shoe Show, The (Brook), 120
*Short Organum for the Theatre
    (Brecht)*, 66, 68, 73, 76, 79, 80
simultaneous dramaturgy,
    144–145
Sistema Coringa, 139
Smug Citizen, The (Gorky), 92
sound, 62–63, 96, 132
spect-actor, 139, 142, 169
Stanislavski, Konstantin, 1–28,
    32, 35, 45, 47, 90, 92, 98, 100,
    104, 111, 138, 155–156

State Institute of Theatre Arts,
    Moscow, 92
State Theatre School, Kraków, 91
Steps (Craig), 42–44
Strasberg, Lee, 6
Stratford-upon-Avon Festival, 113
street scene, 74
subtext, 26–27
supertask, 25, 27
Surrealiste Bureau de
    Recherches, 50
surrealists, 50, 56
synthesis, 72

Tairov, Alexander, 92
*Taming of the Shrew
    (Shakespeare)*, 130, 132
task, 26
Teatro Artístico do Rio de
    Janeiro, O, 137
Teatro de Arena, São Paulo, 138,
    139, 140
Teatro Jornal, 140
Tempest, The (Shakespeare), 114
tempo-rhythm, 21–24
Terry, Ellen, 29, 30, 31
Theater am Schiffbauerdamm, 66
Theaterarbeit (Brecht), 84
*Theatre and its Double, The
    (Artaud)*, 51
theatre as discourse, 147–152
theatre as language, 143–147
Theatre of 13 Rows, Opole, 92
theatre of cruelty, 50, 51, 53,
    55–63, 64, 114, 118–120
Theatre of Nations, Wroclaw, 93
theatre of productions, 92
theatre of sources, 93
theatre of the oppressed, 140,
    141, 141–152, 170
theatre-in-education, 81
thesis, 72
Théâtre Alfred Jarry, 50
Théâtre de l'Oeuvre, 49
Théâtre des Folies-Wagram, 51
Théâtre du Vieux Colombier, 52

Théâtre Sarah Bernhardt, 52
Thévenin, Paule, 52
Thomas, Collette, 52
*Thousand Scenes in One Scene,
The* (Craig), 44
Three Sisters (Chekhov), 4, 25
*Threepenny Opera (Brecht/
Pabst)*, 50
Threepenny Opera, The (Brecht), 65
through-action, 25–26
Thyestes (Seneca), 51
*Timon d'Athènes (Shakespeare/
Carrière)*, 116
Tiradentes (Boal), 139
Titus Andronicus (Shakespeare),
114
*To Have Done with the Judgement
of God (Artaud)*, 52, 57
Tolstoi, Leo, 138
Toulouse, Dr Edward, 49
*Towards A Poor Theatre
(Grotowski)*, 95, 97, 98
Tragédie de Carmen, La, 116
Tsar Fiodor Ioannovich (Tolstoi), 2

Un Chien Andalou (Buñuel), 50
Uncle Vanya (Chekhov), 92
University of California-Irvine, 93
US (Brook), 114, 115
Über-Marionette, 32, 39, 40, 41

Vakhtangov, Evgeni, 3, 92
Van Gogh, Vincent, 52
*Van Gogh, 'suicided' by society
(Artaud)*, 52
Vatermord (Bronnen), 65
Venice Preserved (Otway), 31
Verfremdung, 75
Verfremdungseffekt, 76
via negativa, 97, 170
Vikings at Helgeland, The (Ibsen),
30
Vitrac, Roger, 50

Wedekind, Frank, 67
Weigel, Helene, 65, 66, 84
Weill, Hurt, 65
Wolford, Lisa, 102
Workcenter of Jerzy Grotowski,
94–95
World War II, 91
Woyzeck (Büchner), 58
Writers' Group, Brooklyn, 138

X-9, 138
Yeats, W B, 45

Young Vic, London, 117

Zumbi (Boal), 139, 140
Zurich Schauspielhaus, 83